STEVE OGAN

BREAKTHROUGH in the BATHROOM

BEAUTY AT THE ALTAR OF SANCTIFICATION, REVELATION & RESTORATION

TABLE OF CONTENTS

1

WHAT HAS THE BATHROOM GOT TO DO WITH BREAKTHROUGH?

01

What has the Bathroom got to do With Breakthrough?

"Those who refuse to drink from the well of knowledge will die of thirst in the desert of ignorance" – **Guinean Proverb.**

This is probably the question on your mind as you flip through the pages of this book. You are not alone. Many people are likewise pondering why they seem to have unending encounters as they turn on the shower to take a bath.

Dr. Myles Monroe of Bahamas once said *"I get a lot of revelations in the bathroom. I don't know why God speaks to me in the bathroom."* Even Dr. Mike Murdock has asked similar questions. He too testified of receiving songs, revelations and divine directions in the bathroom.

POINTS TO PONDER ON THE BATHROOM

Why is the voice of the Lord evident in the Bathroom? Why does God wait until one gets into the bathtub to remind us of things we have forgotten? Is there anything special about the bathroom that we have not hitherto known? What is this power that activates the healing virtues in the bathroom? Why is the power universally present in most bathrooms from Boston to Bombay and from Cairo to Calcutta? Why is it evident from New York to New Jersey and from Jerusalem to Jamaica?

The bathroom is obviously not just a place of cleaning our dirty bodies. There must be a spiritual, if not a scientific, explanation of why the spirit of praise and worship often envelops us whenever we are taking a bath. Some people have testified that the spirit of prayer and supplication also comes upon them in the bathroom. Others say that they have received breakthrough ideas in their bath tubs. What has the bathroom got to do with breakthrough? How can we appropriate many more breakthroughs in the bathroom through deeper knowledge and understanding of what goes on there?

We shall attempt to provide answers to these and many more questions. Suffice it to say that there is indeed a divine presence in the bathroom beyond what the ordinary mind can comprehend.

DIVINE SURGERY IN THE BATHROOM

Theresa was pregnant, but in course of one of her antenatal visits to the hospital the doctor discovered that the baby in her womb was growing side by side with a massive fibroid. It was not very clear if she would be able to deliver the baby without the removal of the fibroid. For fear of endangering Theresa's life and that of her unborn baby, the doctor booked her for

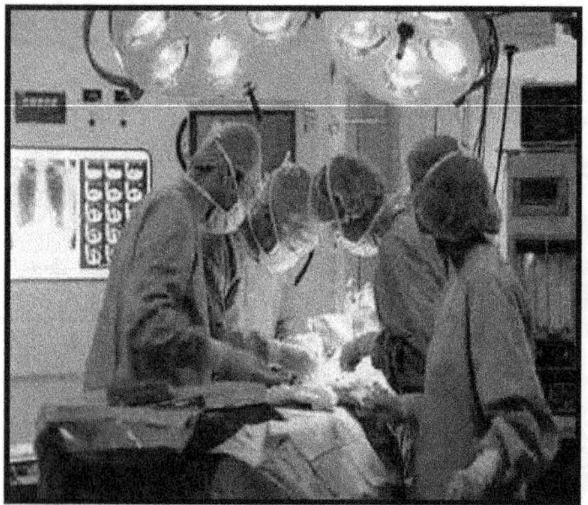

surgery one month after she miraculously delivered safely.

Before the scheduled date for surgery was due, Theresa went to the bathroom to take a bath. Just as she was undressing, God instructed her to get a bucket and urinate in it. This sounded strange. *"Why should I be urinating in a bucket when there is a toilet bowl?"* she asked herself. But the voice she heard became more urgent and persistent. Theresa obeyed the Lord even though she still struggled in her mind.

As she got the bucket and sat on it, Theresa heard the voice of the Lord a second time, *"My daughter, push, push, push!"* Still bewildered, Theresa asked, *"Push what?"* The Lord answered and said, *"I want to do the operation by Myself…"*

Encouraged by the overwhelming divine presence in the bathroom, Theresa pushed three times as she was instructed. At the third push, a very big fibroid came out of her body. The Lord did the fibroid surgery Himself in the theatre of Theresa's bathroom as He had promised.

Meling Elisabeth, a Cameroonian Lady, testified of a similar deliverance from fibroid in the bathroom. After a prayer vigil on Friday night, Elisabeth went to ease herself in the bathroom. She heard the Lord say, *"Urinate on the pissepot and not in the water-closet"*. According to Elisabeth, *"When I finished urinating, I discovered that there were traces of blood with a massive meat-like object."* It was when she visited her cousin that Elisabeth was informed that what came out of her in the bathroom was a fibroid.

There is certainly more to the bathroom than the ordinary eye can comprehend. Get ready to have incredible divine encounters in your bathroom as the Lord unveils the scriptural explanation of why the bathroom is so special. Believe God for deeper dimensions of fellowship and intimacy with the Lord as you catch a revelation of the bathroom as an altar of sanctification, revelation and restoration.

2 | CONCEPT OF THE BATHROOM AS AN ALTAR

02

Concept of the
Bathroom as an Altar

*"Though you wash your cloths with hot water, you still have
to dry them in the Sun"* – **Cameroonian Proverb.**

The family is an altar. This altar sustains life and within it are at least three other altars. These include the altars in the bedroom, the kitchen and the bathroom. In our book *Raising Rainbow Kitchen Initiatives*, we examined how families can appropriate the power at the altar of their kitchens. We proved that the kitchen is an altar for the preservation of life, that those who function at this altar are priests in the kitchen-place and that ministry at this altar is not radically different from ministry at the altar of the local church where priests "cook" spiritual "meals" for the preservation of their congregations.

IGNORANCE OF THE PROPHETIC
SIGNIFICANCE OF THE BATHROOM

Of the three altars in every home, the least recognised and respected is the altar in the bathroom. This is surprising, given the fact that the bathroom is used daily in every family, sometimes three or more times in a twenty-four-hour period. It is amazing that although many people receive daily divine encounters in the bathroom, these spiritual encounters are easily forgotten or neglected. Some people actually think that the flashes of inspiration or insights in the bathroom are coincidental. Others feel that their minds are merely playing tricks on them. Yet others who recognise that there is something special about the bathroom do not really know why this seemingly inconsequential segment of the home is after all so special. *"They know not, neither will they understand; they walk on in darkness: all the foundations of the earth are out of course"* (Psalm 82:5).

Ignorance of the prophetic place of the bathroom in every home is partly responsible for the way little investment is made in the design and construction of many bathrooms. Most bathrooms are like pigeon-holes,

small, sequestrated and side-lined in the scheme of things. The furniture in them is usually bare or non-existent. Even families that have beautiful bathrooms with state-of-the-arts furniture do not really see the significance of this vital segment of every home in spiritual terms.

It is against this background that we need greater divine insight into the prophetic significance of the bathroom and the process of taking a bath. The bathroom is not just a place where you go to clean your body or remove waste matter. It is not merely a place where you brush your teeth or dress up to look beautiful. There is more to the bathroom than meets the ordinary eye. The bathroom is a powerful altar for daily divine encounters with the Holy Spirit. The bathroom is a special place of communion and communication with God. The bathroom is an altar of revelation, restoration and sanctification.

THE BATHROOM AS AN ALTAR

An altar is a meeting place of spirits and man for the purpose of exchanging information and making covenants. It can be a demonic altar raised by satanic agents. It can also be a divine altar raised for the communion of men with the Holy Spirit. Every bathroom is supposed to be a place of communion and communication between individuals, families and God. Although this is not always the case, the general principle is that God wants to interact and speak with His people everywhere, especially at the point of taking a bath.

Have you noticed that there is a spirit of praise and worship that comes upon you whenever you enter the bathroom to take a bath? This is not ordinary! Every altar is a place of worship. Consequently, even though many people have not recognised the bathroom as a worship centre, the Holy Spirit moves them to worship there, their ignorance notwithstanding.

Have you also noticed that God gives you specific instructions in the bathroom? This is because every altar is a spiritual highway of communication between spirits and man. Everything that happens at every other type of altar can be identified with the altar in the bathroom. God is worshipped, revelation is received, restoration is experienced, the heavens are opened, divine insights are given and fresh covenants are cut and old ones renewed.

The time has come to recognise the bathroom as a place of close encounters of the first class. So repent of despising the altar in your bathroom. Realise that destinies have been lost and divine insights jettisoned because of our ignorance of the prophetic nature of the bathroom. It is time to restore the place of the bathroom in your life. It is time to acknowledge the indispensability of the bathroom in the ministry of your family. This can be done when you catch a fresh revelation of the nature of altars in relation to the altar in your bathroom.

NATURE OF ALTARS

Every altar, including the altar in the bathroom, is:

- **A Place of Worship:** *"And the LORD appeared unto Abram, and said, Unto thy seed will I give this land: and there builded he an altar unto the LORD, who appeared unto him. And he removed from thence unto a mountain on the east of Bethel, and pitched his tent, having Bethel on the west, and Hai on the east: and there he builded an altar unto the LORD, and called upon the name of the LORD"* (Genesis 12:7-8).

- **A Place of Communion and Communication between Spirits and Man:** *"And he said unto him, Take me an heifer of three years old, and a she goat of three years old, and a ram of three years old, and a turtledove, and a young pigeon. And he took unto him all these, and divided them in the midst, and laid each piece one against another: but the birds divided he not. And when the fowls came down upon the carcases, Abram drove them away. And when the sun was going down, a deep sleep fell upon Abram; and, lo, an horror of great darkness fell upon him. And he said unto Abram, Know of a surety that*

thy seed shall be a stranger in a land that is not theirs, and shall serve them; and they shall afflict them four hundred years; And also that nation, whom they shall serve, will I judge: and afterward shall they come out with great substance … In the same day the LORD made a covenant with Abram, saying, Unto thy seed have I given this land, from the river of Egypt unto the great river, the river Euphrates" (Genesis 15:9-14,18).

- **A Place of Making Personal and Generational Covenants:** *"And he builded an altar there, and called upon the name of the LORD and pitched his tent there: and there Isaac's servants digged a well. Then Abimelech went to him from Gerar, and Ahuzzath one of his friends, and Phichol the chief captain of his army. And Isaac said unto them, Wherefore come ye to me, seeing ye hate me, and have sent me away from you? And they said, We saw certainly that the LORD was with thee: and we said, Let there be now an oath betwixt us, even betwixt us and thee, and let us make a covenant with thee; That thou wilt do us no hurt, as we have not touched thee, and as we have done unto thee nothing but good, and have sent thee away in peace: thou art now the blessed of the LORD. And he made them a feast, and they did eat and drink. And they rose up betimes in the morning, and sware one to another: and Isaac sent them away, and they departed from him in peace"* (Genesis 26:25-31).

- **A Place of Making Sacrifices:** *"And Noah builded an altar unto the LORD; and took of every clean beast, and of every clean fowl, and offered burnt offerings on the altar. And the LORD smelled a sweet savour; and the LORD said in his heart, I will not again curse the ground any more for man's sake; for the imagination of man's heart is evil from his youth; neither will I again smite any more everything living, as I have done."* (Genesis 8:20-21).

- **A Spiritual Highway Linking Earth to Heaven and Vice Versa:** *"And Jacob went out from Beer-sheba, and went toward Haran … And he dreamed, and behold a ladder set up on the earth, and the top of it reached to heaven: and behold the angels of God ascending and descending on it. And, behold, the LORD stood above it, and said, I am the LORD God of Abraham thy father, and* *the God of Isaac: the land whereon thou liest, to thee will I give it, and to thy seed"* (Genesis 28:10, 12-13).

- **A Place for Accessing Power for the Control of Spiritual Destinies:** *"And, behold, there came a man of God out of Judah by the word of the LORD unto Bethel: and Jeroboam stood by the altar to burn incense. And he cried against the altar in the word of the LORD, and said, O altar, altar, thus saith the LORD; Behold, a child shall be born unto the house of David, Josiah by name; and upon thee shall he offer the priests · of the high places that burn incense upon thee, and men's bones shall be burnt upon thee … And it came to pass, when king Jeroboam heard the saying of the man of God, which had cried against the altar in Bethel, that he put forth his hand from the altar, saying, Lay hold on him. And his hand, which he put forth against him, dried up, so that he could not pull it in again to him. The altar also was rent, and the ashes poured out from the altar, according to the sign which the man of God had given by the word of the LORD. And the king answered and said unto the man of God, Intreat now the face of the LORD thy God, and pray for me, that my hand may be restored me again. And the man of God besought the LORD, and the king's hand was restored him again, and became as it was before"* (1 Kings 13:1-2, 4-6).

- **A Place of Prophetic Proclamations:** *"And he removed from thence, and digged another well; and for that they strove not: and he called the name of it Rehoboth; and he said, For now the LORD hath made room for us, and we shall be fruitful in the land … And he builded an altar there, and called upon the name of the LORD and pitched his tent there: and there Isaac's servants digged a well"* (Genesis 26:22, 25).

- **A Centre of Spiritual Legislation:** *"And Noah builded an altar unto the LORD; and took of every clean beast, and of every clean fowl, and offered burnt offerings on the altar. And the LORD smelled a sweet savour; and the LORD said in his heart, I will not again curse the ground any more for man's sake; for the imagination of man's heart is evil from his youth; neither will I again smite any more everything living, as I have done. While the earth remaineth, seedtime and harvest, and cold and heat, and summer and winter, and day and night shall not cease"* (Genesis 8:20-22).

- **A Place for Making Vows:** *"And Jacob rose up early in the morning, and took the stone that he had put for his pillows, and set it up for a pillar, and poured oil upon the top of it. And he called the name of that place Bethel: but the name of that city was called Luz at the first. And Jacob vowed a vow, saying, If God will be with me, and will keep me in this way that I go, and will give me bread to eat, and raiment to put on, So that I come again to my father's house in peace; then shall the LORD be my God: And this stone, which I have set for a pillar, shall be God's house: and of all that thou shalt give me I will surely give the tenth unto thee"* (Genesis 28:18-22). (Source: Ogan Steve, TPMC Intermediate Manual, pp.68-70).

ENCOUNTER THAT LED TO THE BIRTH OF A MINISTRY

Dr. B. U. Okafor is a medical doctor, an entrepreneur and a minister of the gospel. He is the vision coordinator of the National Evangelism Christian Outreach (NECO). One day, he was taking his bath and God spoke to him at the point of cleaning the water on his body with a towel. God said, *"My children know how to do their own business but they don't know how to do my own work."*

God reminded Dr. Okafor of how he sent out young men and women on National Youth Service Corp with flyers into the neighbourhoods to advertise the new school he and his family were starting. They slipped pieces of paper under the doors of many homes encouraging them to send their children to enrol in the new school. This strategy was so effective that the school took off without much stress.

This is obviously what God was referring to in the bathroom when He reminded Dr. Okafor that we know how to do our own business but not His work of soul-winning. It was this loving rebuke that provoked Dr. Okafor to hire Bible School students on holidays for the task of personal evangelism. The students were given a stipend for doing the work which eventually helped them when school resumed. They went with gospel tracts and spoke the word to people on the streets and in their homes. This was how the National Evangelism Christian Outreach was born. God's divine idea in the bathroom led to the birth of a ministry dedicated to the fulfilment of the Great Commission.

To the ordinary mind, the bathroom is just a place to take a bath. In God's view, however, the bathroom can be much more than a place to clean one's body. It is a worship centre, a spiritual highway and an altar for accessing power and controlling spiritual destinies. The bathroom is a place for making prophetic proclamations and enacting spiritual legislations. It can also be a place for making vows and attracting divine favours at critical times in one's life.

3 | PROPHECY ON BATHROOMS AND BATHING IN THE END-TIME

03

Prophecy on Bathrooms and Bathing in the End-time

The end time is a season of fresh insights and great revelations. It is a time for the restoration of divine truths abandoned at the altars of the apostate church. It will witness the preaching of the gospel of the Kingdom in all nations and spheres of life in preparation for the second coming of the Lord Jesus. Matthew 24:14 declares, *"…this gospel of the kingdom shall be preached in all the world for a witness unto all nations; and then shall the end come."*

The end time is a period of great mind-set transformation. People will experience *"a radical change of mind, action and direction."* This trend of repentance will lead to the restoration of Kingdom patterns. *"And it shall come to pass, that whosoever shall call on the name of the Lord shall be saved"* (Acts 2:21). We are in the season for the restoration of all things which God has spoken by the mouth of all His holy prophets since the world began. An indispensible part of the restoration of all things will involve deeper dimensions of communion and communication with the Holy Spirit, especially at the altar in the bathroom.

PROPHETIC DIRECTION IN THE BATHROOM

God spoke to me specifically about the above reality on the 26th of January 2011 in Abuja, the capital city of Nigeria. The Lord said that *"The bathroom will be one of the greatest places of divine encounters for individuals and couples."*

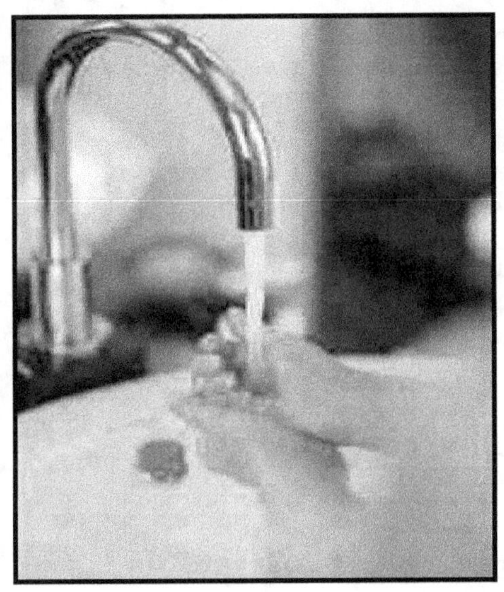

The Lord, as a mighty rushing wind, will come to you in the bathroom. God, as a still small voice, will visit His people in the place of their physical cleansing and purification. The Lord will give divine direction to His people to help them decode hard sentences. He will unveil the covering cast over individuals, families and nations. The bathroom will be a spiritual classroom for receiving divine instructions. It will be a place of the deep calling to the deep. Don't be afraid when you hear the voice of the Lord in the spiritually auspicious environment of your bathroom. The Word of the Lord will come to you as never before. You will hear the Lord saying, *"This is the way to go."*

ANGELIC VISITATIONS AND MIRACULOUS HEALINGS IN THE BATHROOM

There will be great angelic visitations in the bathroom. There will be miraculous encounters as the shower runs its healing virtues on your body. The depressed will be delivered. The sick will be healed, the oppressed will be set free and a mighty miraculous wave will be seen in this hitherto ordinary place with a new extraordinary significance.

The consecrated bathroom will become a spiritual magnet for all who desire deeper dimensions of fellowship with God. Going to the bathroom will no longer be a routine act. It will become a special spiritual phenomenon. Taking a bath will go beyond the desire of people to physically clean their bodies. It will include a passion to see old mind-sets changed into transformed outlooks. The physical washing with water will become the prophetic action that will instigate the washing of the mind by the water of the Word.

SENSITIVITY TO THE PROMPTING OF THE HOLY SPIRIT TO TAKE A BATH

Don't be surprised if the Holy Spirit propels you to take a bath even when you have no need for physical cleansing. Do not resist the prompting to fellowship with the Lord at the altar of your bathroom. Many people will hear the voice of the Lord in the bathroom saying, *"Come up hither and I will show you things that will take place hereafter."* The prophetic word will be heard from the altar of many bathrooms. Divine patterns for solving intricate problems will be unveiled as you look up to the Lord under the shower.

Many people will encounter the unveiling of rainbow colours in their bathtubs. This will be a prophetic signal of God's covenant of divine preservation for the family. It will be a divine signal of the visitation of beauty and balance for God's people.

BREAKDOWN OF THE PROPHECY ON BATHROOMS AND BATHING

1. Bathrooms will be great places of divine encounters. The Lord, as a mighty rushing wind, will come to you in your bathroom.

2. The Holy Spirit, as the still small voice, will visit people as they physically clean and purify themselves. God's people will receive divine directions to decode hard sentences in their bathroom.

3. God will unveil the covering cast over individuals, families and nations. The Bathroom will become a spiritual classroom for receiving divine instructions.

4. The deep will call unto the deep at the altar in the bathroom. Don't be afraid when you hear the voice of the Lord in the bathroom.

5. The Word of the Lord will come to you in the bathroom as never before. You will hear the Lord saying, "This is the way to go."

6. There will be great angelic visitations in the bathroom. There will be miraculous encounters as the shower runs its healing virtues on your spirit, soul and body.

7. The depressed will be delivered, the sick will be healed, and the oppressed will be set free in the bathroom. A mighty miraculous wave will be seen in this hitherto ordinary place with a new extraordinary significance.

8. The consecrated bathroom will become a spiritual magnet for all who desire a deeper dimension of fellowship with God. Going to the bathroom will no longer be a routine act. It will become a special spiritual phenomenon.

9. Taking a bath will go beyond the desire of people to physically clean their bodies. It will include a passion to see old mind sets changed into transformed outlooks. The physical washing with water will become the prophetic action that will instigate the washing of the mind by the water of the Word.

10. Don't be surprised if the Holy Spirit propels you to take a bath even when you have no need for physical cleansing. Do not resist the prompting to fellowship with the Lord at the altar of your bathroom.

11. Many people will hear the voice of the Lord in the bathroom saying, *"Come up hither and I will show you things that will take place hereafter."* The prophetic word will be heard from the altar of many bathrooms.

12. Divine patterns for solving intricate problems will be unveiled as you look up to the Lord under the shower. Many people will encounter the unveiling of rainbow colours in the bathtub. This will be a prophetic signal of God's covenant of preservation. It will be a divine signal of the visitation of beauty and balance for God's people.

Several individuals can already testify to the fulfilment of these words of prophecy. They have fantastic stories of close encounters with the Holy Spirit in their bathrooms. We shall later examine their testimonies with a view to illustrating that there is indeed beauty and breakthrough at the altar of the bathroom. It will suffice to note, now, that whatever divine encounters people have had in the bathroom in the past is nothing compared to the divine visitation awaiting them at this end-time altar of revelation, restoration and progressive sanctification.

4 | THE HOLY SPIRIT AND THE BATHROOM

04

The Holy Spirit and The Bathroom

"A toad will realise the importance of water only when the pond gets dry" – **Zambian Proverb.**

There is a wonderful relationship between the element called water, the personality known as the Holy Spirit and the altar in the bathroom. We cannot fully appreciate the beauty and breakthrough associated with the bathroom without the Holy Spirit and how He is connected with water.

Water is a liquid substance with which the world was created by God. In fact, 75% of the world is made up of water. Similarly, a greater percentage of the human body , about 70%, is also made of water. The first substance mentioned in Scripture is water. Interestingly, water is mentioned in connection with the Holy Spirit. All these have implications for appreciating the prophetic purpose of the bathroom as an altar.

FIRST MENTION OF WATER AND THE HOLY SPIRIT IN SCRIPTURE

The first mention of water and the Holy Spirit in the Bible is in Genesis 1:2, *"And the earth was without form, and void; and darkness was upon the face of the deep. And the Spirit of God moved upon the face of the waters."* The earth at the point of creation had three problems.

1. **Formlessness:** A state of shapelessness which did not allow the earth to have the divine character God intended for it.

2. **Voidness:** A state of emptiness which left a vacuum that needed to be divinely filled.

3. **Darkness:** A state of ignorance which depicted the lack of capacity to comprehend and retain knowledge, understanding and wisdom.

The manifestation of the Holy Spirit on the waters was needed to trigger the resolution of these three dimensional problems. The Holy Spirit first hovered over the face of the waters before God the Father made the proclamation *"Let there be light"*. Then was activated the creative instincts of the pre-incarnate Jesus, by whom light and every other thing in nature was created. The process of creation began with the Holy Spirit hovering over the waters before the problems of formlessness, emptiness and

darkness on earth were dealt with. This implies that even for human beings, there can be a deep relationship between taking a bath and resolving physical, spiritual and emotional problems. There is a close connection between washing with water and activating the process by which problems are solved.

The relationship between taking a bath and receiving divine direction is a mystery. The link between washing with physical water and activating a revelation from the water of God's Word to resolve a crisis is something the carnal mind can never comprehend. There is beauty and breakthrough in the bathroom. Those who do not know and acknowledge the grace of our Lord Jesus Christ and the power of the Holy Spirit cannot appreciate this good news. *"But if our gospel be hid, it is hid to them that are lost: In whom the god of this world hath blinded the minds of them which believe not, lest the light of the glorious gospel of Christ, who is the image of God, should shine unto them"* (2 Corinthians 4:3-4).

WATER AS A SYMBOL OF THE HOLY SPIRIT AND THE MIRACULOUS

The bathroom is an altar of divine breakthroughs partly because the water used in it is symbolic of the Holy Spirit and the Word of God. The Holy Spirit will be present wherever there is consecrated water. Similarly, the power of God's creativity will be activated whenever Jesus, the One by whom all things were made, is allowed to reign.

Remember that Jesus began His public ministry by going to the waters of the Jordan to be baptised. Notice also that the Holy Spirit appeared in the form of a dove at this first recorded encounter of Jesus with a body of water. Jesus came up out of the water praying and several miraculous things began to happen at the Jordan.

First, *"…it came to pass that Jesus also was baptised. And while He prayed the heaven was opened. And the Holy Spirit descended in bodily form like a dove upon Him, and a voice came from heaven which said, "you are my beloved son, in you I am well pleased"* (Luke 3:21-22). Secondly, *"When he had been baptised, Jesus came up immediately from the water; and behold the heavens were opened to Him and He saw the Spirit of God descending like a dove and alighting upon Him"* (Matthew 3:16).

THE POWER OF TAKING A SPIRIT-LED BATH

The combined accounts of the Baptism of Jesus in Matthew and Luke reveal that the presence of water, the Holy Spirit and Jesus at the River Jordan activated a string of miraculous events.

- Prayer was activated at the waters of the Jordan when Jesus took the spiritual bath called baptism.

- The heavens were opened for fresh revelation of God's plans and purposes.

- The Holy Spirit descended in bodily form like a dove and alighted on Jesus.

- The voice of God the Father from Heaven was heard audibly.

- There was a public recognition of Jesus by His father as *"My beloved Son in whom I am well pleased."*

- There was a spirit of urgency activated because *"Jesus came up immediately from the water."*

- Divine ability to see in the realm of the spirit was released as Jesus *"…saw the Spirit of God descending like a dove."*

- There was a divine touch, a spirit-generated anointing, as the Holy Spirit alighted upon Jesus.

- There was a proof-producing testimony as Jesus overcame the temptations of the Devil in the wilderness.

A WORD FOR THOSE WHO DESIRE TO
TAKE SPIRIT-LED BATHS

Turn every bathing time into periods of spiritual encounter. As you do so, the Spirit of grace and supplication will be activated on the waters of your bathroom. The heavens will be opened to you for fresh revelation of God's plans and purposes for you, your family and for the nations.

The Holy Spirit will descend in multidimensional forms. He will alight upon your spirit, soul and body. He will touch you as no one else could ever. You will hear the voice of the Lord from Heaven giving you direction, acknowledging the right paths you have taken and warning you of wrong moves that could devastate your destiny.

The zeal of the Lord will consume you from the altar of the bathroom. A new spirit of urgency will come upon you, as you come out of your bathtub. You will be activated and energised to do the things you could not do before. The power to deal with procrastination will be released to you. You will receive the divine enablement to do in three and a half years what you could not do in thirty years. God's grace will be unleashed for you to do in a short time what you could not do for a very long time.

The eyes of your understanding will be enlightened as the water of God's Word anoints your eyes to see things in the realm of the spirit. You will receive a divine ability to do the things you could not do before. A veil will be torn for the visions of glory to be revealed to you. A new divine touch is coming upon you. A fresh spirit-generated anointing will come on you.

You will become a proof-producer, able to overcome temptations in every wilderness of your life.

PRACTICAL PROCLAMATIONS IN THE BATHROOM

Turn the above word of prophecy into a personal proclamation in your bathroom. Make this declaration, *"I invite the Holy Spirit into the altar of this bathroom. I sanctify the water in my bathtub and in the shower by the blood of Jesus. I activate the spirit of grace and supplication in my life. I declare that the grace to pray is upon me. I receive power to deal with anything that represents formlessness, voidness and darkness in my life and in my family.*

Let the heavens be opened to me for fresh revelation of God's plans and purposes. Let the Holy Spirit descend upon me. I receive the touch and the anointing of the Holy Ghost. I activate the voice of the Lord for definite direction and divine insight. I will never be confused. I will never be lost. The Lord is my light and my salvation. The Lord is my way even in the wilderness. I will not walk in the counsel of the ungodly. I will not stand in the path of sinners; nor sit in the seat of the scornful. I will delight in the law of the Lord, especially at the altar of my bathroom. I will meditate on God's law day and night. I am like a tree planted by the rivers of water. I will bring forth fruits in season and out of season. My leaves also shall not wither and whatever I do will prosper.

"The zeal of the Lord will consume me from the altar of my bathroom; the spirit of urgency will come upon me. God will do a quick work in me. He will use me to do a quick work for His kingdom. I reject procrastination, I renounce laziness and lukewarmness. I receive the grace to do in a short time what I have not been able to do for a long time.

The eyes of my understanding are enlightened. My eyes are anointed with eye-salve. I can see in the realm of the spirit. I can comprehend God's plans and purposes. The touch of the Holy Spirit is upon me and I am anointed to produce proof that the Holy Spirit is my guide, the Lord Jesus is my saviour and the Father is my source."

EIGHT SPIRIT-ACTIVATED MIRACLES ON WATER

1. **Light was Generated as the Holy Spirit Hovered on the Waters at the Point of Creation:** *"In the beginning God created the heaven and the earth. And the earth was without form, and void; and darkness was upon the face of the deep. And the Spirit of God moved upon the face of the waters. And God said, Let there be light: and there was light"* (Genesis 1:1-3).

2. **Bitter Water was made Sweet at Marah:** *"So Moses brought Israel from the Red sea, and they went out into the wilderness of Shur; and they went three days in the wilderness, and found no water. And when they came to Marah, they could not drink of the waters of Marah, for they were bitter: therefore the name of it was called Marah. And the people murmured against Moses, saying, What shall we drink? And he cried unto the LORD; and the LORD shewed him a tree, which when he had cast into the waters, the waters were made sweet: there he made for them a statute and an ordinance, and there he proved them"* (Exodus 15:22-25).

3. **The Waters of Jordan were Divided for Israel to Cross Over to the Promised Land:** *"And it came to pass, when the people removed from their tents, to pass over Jordan, and the priests bearing the ark of the covenant before the people; And as they that bare the ark were come unto Jordan, and the feet of the priests that bare the ark were dipped in the brim of the water, (for Jordan overfloweth all his banks all the time of harvest,) That the waters which came down from above stood and rose up upon an heap very far from the city Adam, that is beside Zaretan: and those that came down toward the sea of the plain, even the salt sea, failed, and were cut off: and the people passed over right against Jericho. And the priests that bare the ark of the covenant of the LORD stood firm on dry ground in the midst of Jordan, and all the Israelites passed over on dry ground, until all the people were passed clean over Jordan"* (Joshua 3:14-17).

4. **Barren Water was Healed to Bring Restoration to the Land:** *"And the men of the city said unto Elisha, Behold, I pray thee, the situation of this city is pleasant, as my lord seeth: but the water is naught, and the ground barren. And he said, Bring me a new cruse, and put salt therein. And they brought it to him. And he went forth unto the spring of the waters, and cast the salt in there, and said, Thus saith the LORD, I have healed these waters; there shall not be from thence any more death or barren land. So the waters were healed unto this day, according to the saying of Elisha which he spake"* (2 Kings 2:19-22).

5. **An Axe Head in Water was made to Float:** *"But as one was felling a beam, the axe head fell into the water: and he cried, and said, Alas, master! for it was borrowed. And the man of God said, Where fell it? And he shewed him the place. And he cut down a stick, and cast it in thither; and the iron did swim. Therefore said he, Take it up to thee. And he put out his hand, and took it"* (2 Kings 6:5-7).

6. **Leprosy was Healed as Naaman Took a Dip in the Water Seven Times:** *"Then went he down, and dipped himself seven times in Jordan, according to the saying of the man of God: and his flesh came again like unto the flesh of a little child, and he was clean"* (2 Kings 5:14).

7. **Jesus Walked on Water to Demonstrate Sovereignty over Nature:** *"But when they saw him walking upon the sea, they supposed it had been a spirit, and cried out: For they all saw him, and were troubled. And immediately he talked with them, and saith unto them, Be of good cheer: it is I; be not afraid. And he went up unto them into the ship; and the wind ceased: and they were sore amazed in themselves beyond measure, and wondered. For they considered not the miracle of the loaves: for their heart was hardened"* (Mark 6:49-52).

8. **Water was Changed to Wine at the Wedding Feast in Cana:** *"Jesus saith unto them, Fill the waterpots with water. And they filled them up to the brim. And he saith unto them, Draw out now, and bear unto the governor of the feast. And they bare it. When the ruler of the feast had tasted the water that was made wine, and knew not whence it was: (but the servants which drew the water knew;) the governor of the feast called the bridegroom, And saith unto him, Every man at the beginning doth set forth good wine; and when men have well drunk, then that which is worse: but thou hast kept the good wine until now"* (John 2:7-10).

Jean-Marie Ghomsi Komkue from Cameroon writes that the *"Bath and toilet rooms are a place of intimacy… isolation… and perfect communication with God."* She says *"I have never seen anyone weeping while bathing. A good bath is the manifestation of the love of God.*

- *Water Cradles you*
- *Water Caresses you*
- *Water Consoles you*
- *Water gives you Joy*
- *Water gives you Peace*
- *Water Teaches you*
- *Water makes you Adjust*
- *Water Bruises the Yoke of Anger*

Jane-Marie further notes that a good bath in spirit and truth gives us the necessary equipment... for winning the wars of life, day and night. Anyone who goes out to work without having a good bath is tired, heavy in executing the task at hand, slow... lazy, demotivated, ill at ease, and out of tune with his environment. On the contrary, anyone who refreshes himself in the bathroom is strong, enthusiastic, trusting, joyful, motivated, encouraging and better able to perform his duties"

There may seem to be slight exaggeration in Jean-Marie's glorification of a good bath. Nevertheless, there is no doubt that she is generally right. Most people who take a good bath are more refreshed and motivated than those who don't. Water indeed cradles, caresses, consoles and gives you joy. Water refreshes, revives and renews you. Water, as Jean-Marie has noted, *"Bruises the yoke of anger"*.

The fact that water has always been associated with the miraculous helps us to understand and appreciate why the process of taking a bath can become a source of beauty and divine breakthrough in the bathroom.

5 | THE THREE WITNESSES OF HEAVEN AND ON EARTH

05

The Three Witnesses of Heaven and on Earth

quote

Wherever the Father is, the Son and the Holy Spirit will be there. Similarly, wherever the Spirit is, the water and the Blood will be there. The presence of water in your bathroom automatically means that the spirit and the Blood are also there. The healings and deliverances people receive in the bathroom is a product of the presence of three powerful witnesses on earth who are spiritually aligned to the three witnesses in heaven – the Father, the Word and the Spirit.

The spirit, the water and the blood combined is a powerful weapon against disease and demonic oppression. Take the blood of Jesus for instance, its efficacy can be seen in the fact that it performs multidimensional functions. Abu Bako in his teaching on the efficacy of the Blood at the 11th International Conference of the Wailing Women in Port Harcourt, Nigeria, declared that the Blood of Jesus is:

1.   The Life-Force of the Universe.

2.   The Password for Access to all Things.

3.   The Highest Currency in the Universe.

4.   The Most-Powerful Title-Deed in Heaven and on Earth.

5.   The Divine Access to Power, Wealth, Wisdom, Strength, Honour, Glory and Power.

6.   Evidence that those who belong to Jesus are no Longer Available for Sale to the Devil.

7.   An Instrument of Judgment against Wicked Individuals, Thrones and Nations.

8.   The Spiritual Magnet for Drawing People to God and to God's Grace.

9.   The Most Powerful Instrument of Detribalisation.

10.   The Foundation of Light and all that it Represents.

11.   The Means for Reconciling Everything Estranged from God.

12.   The Access to the Storehouse of Heaven for the Benefit of Earth's Citizens.

Wherever water is present so also is the blood and the spirit. The bathroom is a reservoir for water. No wonder, it is also an altar of sanctification, revelation and restoration – a place of power to deliver and to heal.

Never enter the bathroom to take your bath without activating the three witnesses on earth. Invoke the grace they carry to activate the miracle working power of the Almighty God. The three witnesses on earth are not just exhibits, they are divine testifiers. This means that they carry a divine personality that cannot be ignored. They testify to the price that Jesus paid on the cross to blot out our transgressions and curses. The spirit of God, the water of the word and the

Blood of Jesus are all life-giving forces. They are always present in each other and they are in perfect agreement at all times. Their presence in your bathroom is responsible for the miraculous, restorations and revivals you have experienced there. This was so even when you did not have a revelation of the prophetic significance of the bathroom. Now that you know, there is no limitation that you cannot break at this altar of grace and glory. The power of God shall rest upon you as you activate the three witnesses that bear record in heaven and on earth.

THE THREE WITNESSES IN HEAVEN AND ON EARTH

S/N	Witnesses in Heaven	Witnesses on Earth
1.	The Father	The Spirit
2.	The Word	The Water
3.	The Holy Spirit	The Blood

"For there are three that bear record in heaven, the Father, the Word, and the Holy Ghost: and these three are one. And there are three that bear witness in earth, the Spirit, and the water, and the blood: and these three agree in one" (1 John 5:7-8).

6 | THE UNIQUE CHARACTER OF THE ALTAR IN THE BATHROOM

06

The Unique Character of
The Altar in the Bathroom

Every altar has its divine identity different from other altars. Different altars may share the general features associated with other centres of worship. Nevertheless, each altar has its own unique identity. The rainbow altar of the kitchen is not exactly the same as the altar of revelation and sanctification in the bathroom.

The bathroom, therefore, can be characterised specifically as an:

1. **Altar of Sanctification and Purification:** It is a place of separating the profane from the holy. It is a place of washing for the purpose of physical and spiritual purification. Waste matters are removed from the bodies of individuals. Dirty bodies are washed and purified physically. But all this has a spiritual implication which goes beyond the common act of washing and cleaning the body. There is a divine link between the physical cleansing of the body and the separation of the mind for a holy use. There is a strong relationship between the ordinary purification of the body by water and the spiritual conditioning of the mind by the water of God's Word. Washing the body can be a prophetic action that opens an individual for the mind to be restored and renewed.

2. **Altar of Revelation and Restoration:** The bathroom is an altar of revelation and restoration. Bernard Isiguzo tells the story of how he entered the bathroom in his home in Jos only to receive the revelation of his transfer to a new work station. The Lord spoke to Bernard that he would be going on transfer while he was taking a bath. He went to the office only for his boss to tell him that he has been transferred to Aba. There was a peace and calmness in him because God had already communicated this information to him. The essence of revelation is to ensure restoration. Taking a bath is the process of restoring the body to a state of cleanliness. There is a relationship between the physical restoration of the body in the bathroom and the spiritual restoration of the spirit and the soul by the Holy Spirit.

3. **Altar of Refreshment and Revival:** Water poured on a tired body does not just refresh and revive the body, it also rejuvenates the spirit and the soul. Everyone can testify to how a calmness and peace envelops them as soon as they take a bath after a hot and humid day of hard  labour. The refreshments and revivals that accompany a bath are not just products of water. The presence of the Holy Spirit in the bathroom and the atmosphere for miracles created there is responsible for the peace that passes all understanding which pervades one's heart after a strategic bath. Just as a dying man is refreshed by water, so the Word of God refreshes and revives a spiritually thirsty soul. Proverbs 25:25 says, *"As cold water to a weary soul, so is good news from a far country."*

4. **Altar of Creativity and Innovation:** Many people testify of receiving songs and prophetic poems in the bathroom. This is because the bathroom is an altar of creativity and innovation. Remember that the whole of creation began when the Holy Spirit hovered over the waters. This was the signal for the creation of light, the firmament, dry land, the sun, moon and stars, the great living creatures in the seas and the plants and animals. There can be no creativity without the divine enablement of the Holy Spirit. One engineer testified that most of his designs are developed in the bathroom. For him, therefore, the bathroom is not just a place to take a bath, but an altar for receiving divine insight for the professional task of designing bridges, roads and instruments for transmitting power. Similarly, I have personally received many book titles and ideas when taking a bath. The concept of *Prophetic Marriages*, the subject of a book published by Destiny Image Europe, was received in the bathroom. It defines marriage as a ministry and couples as being on assignment. It also conceives marital relationships in the context of marriage to the land, Eunuch-type marriages and the union of widows with the Lord. There is no doubt that the creative instincts of other writers have been activated in the altar of the bathroom.

5. **Altar of Renewal and Beautification:** The bathroom is an altar of renewal. Every time you enter there and come out, your spirit, soul and body are renewed. It is also the altar of beautification. This is why many women spend a long time in the bathroom. They want to be beautified. Unfortunately, many people think in terms of physical beauty and not the beauty of holiness. Others are more concerned with physical renewal and not the more important dimension of spiritual renewal of covenant relationships. Henceforth, however, begin to see your times in the bathroom as moments of covenant renewal. See it as times of purification for the purpose of experiencing the beauty of holiness.

6. **Altar of Covenant Remembrance:** The bathroom is a powerful altar where the Holy Spirit reminds you of things you have forgotten. It is a place of covenant remembrance. When I was doing the research for this book, I asked Joy, one of my daughters in Aba, to give me any testimonies of divine encounters in the bathroom. She did not initially remember any such testimonies, even with all the efforts she made. But as soon as she entered the bathroom and began to take her bath, the Lord reminded her of a definite testimony of a man of God who received a revelation on what to do to resolve a crisis in his marriage while taking a bath. Remember that the Holy Spirit is present in any body of sanctified and purified water. The times of washing with water will remind you of all things.

It was at Beersheba, also known as the "Well of the Oath", that God reminded Isaac of the covenant He had with his father Abraham. *"Then he went up from there to Beersheba. And the Lord appeared to him the same night and said, I am the God of your father Abraham do not fear, for I am with you. I will bless you and multiply your descendants for my servant Abraham's sake. So he built an altar there and called on the name of the Lord, and he pitched his tent there; and there Isaac's servants dug a well"* (Genesis 26:23-25).

CONSECRATE YOUR BATHROOM AS A PLACE OF COVENANT REMEMBRANCE

Beersheba was already an altar before Isaac had a divine encounter there and raised yet another altar. It was a well and this probably provoked God to appear to Isaac there. Consecrate your bathroom as a place of covenant. Turn it into another Beersheba.

Beersheba was a place of covenant remembrance, divine reassurance and exceeding multiplication. It was a place of refreshment, an altar of communion and communication with God. Beersheba was a secure dwelling place for Isaac and his family. It also turned out to be a place where Isaac's enemies were compelled to make peace with him because they saw that the Lord was with him. It was at Beersheba that Abimelech, king of Gerar, who hated Isaac, came to make peace with him. *"Then Abimelech went to him from Gerar, and Ahuzzath one of his friends, and Phichol the chief captain of his army. And Isaac said unto them, Wherefore come ye to me, seeing ye hate me, and have sent me away from you? And they said, We saw certainly that the LORD was with thee: and we said, Let there be now an oath betwixt us, even betwixt us and thee, and let us make a covenant with thee; That*

thou wilt do us no hurt, as we have not touched thee, and as we have done unto thee nothing but good, and have sent thee away in peace: thou art now the blessed of the LORD. And he made them a feast, and they did eat and drink. And they rose up betimes in the morning, and sware one to another: and Isaac sent them away, and they departed from him in peace" (Genesis 26:26-31).

Your bathroom can be a place of covenant remembrance. It can be an altar of divine reassurance. You too can hear God say, *"Fear not, for I am with you. I will bless you and multiply your descendants… for my sake"*. Your bathroom can be a place of security, a platform for compelling your enemies to be at peace with you because your ways please God. The Scripture says that *"When a man's ways pleases God, He makes his enemies to be at peace with him"* (Proverbs 16:7). Create an atmosphere in your bathroom that will help you to be at peace with the Lord and He will make your enemies to be at peace with you.

7 | THE MIRACLE OF OPEN HEAVEN IN THE BATHROOM

07

The Miracle of Open Heaven
in the Bathroom

"Shortcuts may carry more traffic than the main road" – **Ugandan Proverb.**

The bathroom is a place where your heavens can be opened perpetually, depending on how you consecrated it and what you do there. The bathroom is a place of divine open heavens. Our ability to hear God clearly is activated there. Your spiritual antennas are sharper and more sensitive.

Ignorance of the prophetic significance of the bathroom has limited the ability of people to appropriate the miracle of open heavens in the bathroom. The water in your bathroom is not ordinary, if you consecrate it and recognise that the Holy Spirit and God's ministering angels are present there to stir it up for your edification and transformation. Every consecrated water is a potential dwelling place of the Holy Spirit and angels. Revelation 17:5 talks of "the angel of the waters". Could it be that the revelations, restorations and renewals experienced under the shower are activated by "the angel of the waters"? Could it be that the numerous testimonies of divine encounters in the bathroom are engineered by these angels in conjunction with the Holy Spirit that hovers over the waters?

We may not be able to categorically answer these questions. Nevertheless, insights from the Scriptures indicate that angels are attracted to water bodies. The heavens have also been known to open around rivers, streams and lakes, when saints are praying and reading Scriptures and when the right scriptural keys are applied by prophetic voices.

EXAMPLES OF OPEN HEAVENS AROUND WATER BODIES

1. **Open Heavens at Creation:** *"In the beginning God created the heaven and the earth. And the earth was without form, and void; and darkness was upon the face of the deep. And the Spirit of God moved upon the face of the waters. And God said, Let there be light: and there was light. And God saw the light, that it was good: and God divided the light from the darkness"* (Genesis 1:1-4).

2. **Open Heavens at the River Chebar:** *"Now it came to pass in the thirtieth year, in the fourth month, in the fifth day of the month, as I was among the captives by the river of Chebar, that the heavens were opened, and I saw visions of God... The word of the LORD came expressly unto Ezekiel the priest, the son of Buzi, in the land of the Chaldeans by the river Chebar; and the hand of the LORD was there upon him"* (Ezekiel 1:1, 3).

3. **Open Heavens at the Baptism of Jesus in River Jordan:** *"Then cometh Jesus from Galilee to Jordan unto John, to be baptized of him... And Jesus, when he was baptized, went up straightway out of the water: and, lo, the heavens were opened unto him, and he saw the Spirit of God descending like a dove, and lighting upon him"* (Matthew 3:16).

4. **Open Heavens at the Seaside in Joppa when Peter was Praying:** *"On the morrow, as they went on their journey, and drew nigh unto the city, Peter went up upon the housetop to pray about the sixth hour: And he became very hungry, and would have eaten: but while they made ready, he fell into a trance, And saw heaven opened, and a certain vessel descending unto him, as it had been a great sheet knit at the four corners, and let down to the earth: Wherein were all manner of fourfooted beasts of the earth, and wild beasts,*

and creeping things, and fowls of the air. And there came a voice to him, Rise, Peter; kill, and eat" (Acts 10:9-13).

5. **Open Heavens after John Received the Seven Letters to the Churches:** *"After this I looked, and, behold, a door was opened in heaven: and the first voice which I heard was as it were of a trumpet talking with me; which said, Come up hither, and I will shew thee things which must be hereafter. And immediately I was in the spirit: and, behold, a throne was set in heaven, and one sat on the throne. And he that sat was to look upon like a jasper and a sardine stone: and there was a rainbow round about the throne, in sight like unto an emerald"* (Revelation 4:1-3).

DEAL WITH THE FORMLESSNESS, EMPTINESS AND DARKNESS AROUND YOU

These examples of open heavens around water bodies can help us to appreciate the necessity to believe God that the heavens can also be opened for us in the bathroom. Before the earth experienced open heavens at creation, it suffered the triple dimensional problems of formlessness, emptiness and darkness. Through the ministry of the Trinity, these problems were overcome. The Holy Spirit hovered over the waters to sanctify them. God the Father made the proclamation, "Let there be light" and the Lord Jesus, by whom all things were created, ensured that there was light. Therein began the six-day creation process through which the problems of shapelessness, emptiness and ignorance were overcome.

You too can overcome similar problems at the altar of your bathroom. Invoke the power of the Holy Spirit to help you overcome formlessness in your life. Activate the creative energy of the Lord Jesus to deal with emptiness in your family. Appropriate the prophetic proclamation of God the Father to drive away every aspect of darkness around you. The power of God is present in your bathroom to heal. The glory of God is available at the altar of restoration in your home.

OVERCOME CAPTIVITY BY DIVINE REVELATION
IN THE BATHROOM

The children of Israel were captives in Babylon. But some of them, including Ezekiel refused to allow their spirits to be taken captive. You may be in one physical captivity or the other. Your health may be down, your finances in shambles and your family in crisis. But you can determine not to allow your spirit to be a captive of Satan and his demons.

Like Ezekiel at the River Chebar, you can enter into the altar of your bathroom, under the overflowing grace in your shower to receive the miracle of open heavens. What you need is "a fresh vision of God's majesty", a revelation of His sovereignty over your situation and faith in His capacity to help you overcome your negative circumstances. Ezekiel was among the captives when the heavens were opened for him to see the visions of God. King Jehoiachin and his fellow countrymen were in captivity on all fronts, but Ezekiel's spirit was free to see the visions of God. Others were by the river with him, but only Ezekiel experienced the miracle of open heavens.

The same bathroom others enter and come out without any special encounters will be the place of your open heavens. The Word of the Lord will come to you expressly in the bathroom. The hand of the Lord will be upon you there for good. Ezekiel was in the place of captivity but saw heavenly creatures, including the throne of God. *"And above the firmament that was over their heads was the likeness of a throne, as the appearance of a sapphire stone: and upon the likeness of the throne was the likeness as the appearance of a man above upon it. And I saw as the colour of amber, as the appearance of fire round about within it, from the appearance of his loins even upward, and from the appearance of his loins even downward, I saw as it were the appearance of fire, and it had brightness round about. As the appearance of the bow that is in the cloud in the day of rain, so was the appearance of the brightness round about. This was the appearance of the likeness of the glory of the LORD. And when I saw it, I fell upon my face, and I heard a voice of one that spake"* (Ezekiel 1:26-28).

The vision of the throne of God and the rainbow around the throne were a prophetic assurance that God will preserve and eventually deliver His people from captivity. Let the altar in your bathroom become the place of divine reassurance. Ask God for the grace to see there what others cannot see. Believe God to show you *"the appearance of the likeness of the glory of the Lord"* in the bathroom even in your moment of captivity.

PRAY TO RECEIVE HEAVEN'S RECOGNITION IN YOUR BATHROOM

An altar is a place of prayer. As Jesus prayed after he was dipped by John the Baptist into the waters of the Jordan, the heavens were opened to him. Several miraculous things happened thereafter. There was a spirit of urgency that moved Jesus to begin his ministry. He saw the Holy Spirit in the form of a dove. The Third Person of the Trinity alighted upon him and God's voice of recognition was heard from Heaven.

You too can have similar experiences in your bathroom. The heavens will be opened to you. You will see visions of God. The Holy Spirit will come upon you. The power of the Highest will overshadow you. You will experience divine conception of a miraculous seed that will lead to the transformation of nations.

A spirit of urgency to fulfil the mandate of God for your life will come upon you as you experience a divine encounter in your bathroom. Like Jesus, you too can immediately begin to do the things that time and tradition may have restricted you from doing. The hand of the Lord will come upon you and you too can become a proof-producer like Jesus.

BE RESTORED TO OVERCOME THE TRADITIONS OF MEN

When the heavens were opened for Peter as he prayed and meditated on the Scriptures, God showed him a vision. Whenever the heavens open, men see visions of God. They receive a divine call and direction for specific ministries appointed for them. It was after the heavens opened at the River Chebar and Ezekiel saw the visions of God that God called him and gave him the mandate for his call. *"And he said unto me, Son of man, stand upon thy feet, and I will speak unto thee. And the spirit entered into me when he spake unto me, and set me upon my feet, that I heard him that spake unto me. And he said unto me, Son of man, I send thee to the children of Israel, to a rebellious nation that hath rebelled against me: they and their fathers have transgressed against me, even unto this very day. For they are impudent children and stiff hearted. I do send thee unto them; and thou shalt say unto them, Thus saith the Lord GOD. And they, whether they will hear, or whether they will forbear, (for they are a rebellious house,) yet shall know that there hath been a prophet among them. And thou, son of man, be not afraid of them, neither be afraid of their words, though briers and thorns be with thee, and thou dost dwell among scorpions: be not afraid of their words, nor be dismayed at their looks, though they be a rebellious house. And thou shalt speak my words unto them, whether they will hear, or whether they will forbear: for they are most rebellious. But thou, son of man, hear what I say unto thee; Be not thou rebellious like that rebellious house: open thy mouth, and eat that I give thee. And when I looked, behold, an hand was sent unto me; and, lo, a roll of a book was therein; And he spread it before me; and it was written within and without: and there was written therein lamentations, and mourning, and woe"* (Ezekiel 2:1-10).

Like Ezekiel, Peter also saw the visions of God after the heavens were opened. *"On the morrow, as they went on their journey, and drew nigh unto the city, Peter went up upon the housetop to pray about the sixth hour: And he became very hungry, and would have eaten: but while they made ready, he fell into a trance, And saw heaven opened, and a certain vessel descending unto him, as it had been a great sheet knit at the four corners, and let down to the earth: Wherein were all manner of fourfooted beasts of the earth, and wild beasts, and creeping things, and fowls of the air. And there came a voice to him, Rise, Peter; kill, and eat. But Peter said, Not so, Lord; for I have never eaten anything that is common or unclean. And the voice spake unto him again the second time, What God hath cleansed, that call not thou common"* (Acts 10:9-15).

Both Peter and Ezekiel may not have answered the call of God if they were not given the details of their call. Notice that because Peter felt that the Gentiles were unclean, he on his own would never have reached out to them with the good news. It took an open rebuke by the Lord during the

encounter with the open heavens for Peter to go to the Gentiles.

There are many things you may not ordinarily do which God will compel you to do as the heavens are opened to you in the bathroom. Usually, when the heavens are opened and saints see the vision of God, the Word of God comes to them expressly. The Word of the Lord is usually so strong that the one receiving it has little or no room to resist the mandate it carries. How else could Ezekiel agree to reach a people so stubborn that they would not repent? Why spend so much time and energy talking to people who are determined to remain in their sins? The fact that the Word of the Lord came to Ezekiel and Peter at various altars made it easier for them to agree to do a difficult assignment which for Peter turned out to be eternally fruitful. *"While Peter was still speaking these words, the Holy Spirit fell upon those who heard the word. And those of the circumcision who believed were astonished, as many came with Peter, because the gift of the Holy Spirit had been poured out on the Gentiles also. For they heard them speak with tongues and magnify God. Then Peter answered, can anyone forbid water, that these should not be baptized who had received the Holy*

Spirit just as we have? And he commanded them to be baptized in the name of the Lord. Then they asked him to say a few days" (Acts 10:44-48).

The altar in your bathroom and the washing of water by the Word must activate a new mind-set in you. Get ready to throw away the traditions of men so that the grace to do the will of God will be bestowed on you. God will do a spiritual surgery in your mind to prepare you to engage in ventures which are Kingdom-based, but which you have hitherto abandoned because of the traditions of men.

GET READY TO RECEIVE INSTRUCTIONS ON THINGS THAT WILL BE HEREAFTER

The altar in the bathroom will be a place where Kingdom models or patterns will be revealed for onward replication on earth. After Jesus dictated the letters to the seven churches in a voice described as "the sound of many waters", the heavens were opened for John. *"After this I looked, and, behold, a door was opened in heaven: and the first voice which I heard was as it were of a trumpet talking with me; which said, Come up hither, and I will shew thee things which must be hereafter. And immediately I was in the spirit: and, behold, a throne was set in heaven, and one sat on the throne"* (Revelation 4:1-2).

John the Beloved was shown the pattern of the thrones that should be replicated on earth. John was shown the rainbow throne of God with His council of Elders, the apostolic and prophetic voices round the throne and the seven spirits of God. This was a vision of thrones that earth's potentates should set up in line with the rainbow throne of God in Heaven. Before God's throne was a golden altar where the prayer of the saints were received, collated and stored in containers or golden censers.

Get ready to receive similar heavenly models for restoring the institutions on earth. The visions of God at the altar of your bathroom will affect the things that happen on earthly thrones. They will affect the patters in the marketplace. They will influence the curriculum in educational institutions. The will of God will be done on earth as we receive the models of Heaven based on the mystery of open heavens.

Stop going to the bathroom as a matter of routine. The Holy Spirit will sometimes propel you to take a bath even when you don't have any need for physical cleansing. God wants to use you to release the things that should be hereafter.

8 | **HOW TO ACTIVATE THE MIRACLE OF OPEN HEAVENS IN YOUR BATHROOM**

08

How to Activate the Miracle of Open Heavens in Your Bathroom

"Digging a well starts from the top though the water is at the bottom" – **Tanzanian Proverb.**

The Holy Spirit and the angels of the waters are waiting to minister to you in the bathroom. You must be fully aware of how to activate them to open the heavens for yourself. Everyone must take personal responsibility to ensure that the heavens are opened. Two people may use the same altar and the heavens can be like brass for one and yet open for the other.

EXPERIENCING OPEN HEAVENS AT THE ALTAR IN YOUR BATHROOM

To experience open heavens in your bathroom, you must:

1. **Set your Affection on the Things Above:** *"If ye then be risen with Christ, seek those things which are above, where Christ sitteth on the right hand of God. Set your affection on things above, not on things on the earth. For ye are dead, and your life is hid with Christ in God"* (Colossians 3:1-3).

2. **Diligently Obey the Voice of the Lord and His Commandments:** *"And it shall come to pass, if thou shalt hearken diligently unto the voice of the LORD thy God, to observe and to do all his commandments which I command thee this day, that the LORD thy God will set thee on high above all nations of*

the earth… The LORD shall open unto thee his good treasure, the heaven to give the rain unto thy land in his season, and to bless all the work of thine hand: and thou shalt lend unto many nations, and thou shalt not borrow" (Deuteronomy 28:1, 12).

3. **Pray without Ceasing, especially in the Spirit:** *"And he from within shall answer and say, Trouble me not: the door is now shut, and my children are with me in bed; I cannot rise and give thee. I say unto you, Though he will not rise and give him, because he is his friend, yet because of his importunity he will rise and give him as many as he needeth. And I say unto you, Ask, and it shall be given you; seek, and ye shall find; knock, and it shall be opened unto you. For every one that asketh receiveth; and he that seeketh findeth; and to him that knocketh it shall be opened"* (Luke 11:7-10).

4. **Appreciate the Due Season Appointed for Open Heavens:** *"For this shall every one that is godly pray unto thee in a time when thou mayest be found: surely in the floods of great waters they shall not come nigh unto him… I will instruct thee and teach thee in the way which thou shalt go: I will guide thee with mine eye"* (Psalms 32:6, 8).

5. **Seek First the Kingdom of God and His Righteousness:** *"But seek ye first the kingdom of God, and his righteousness; and all these things shall be added unto you"* (Matthew 6:33).

6. **Pay your Tithes and Give Generous Free-will Offerings:** *"Bring ye all the tithes into the storehouse, that there may be meat in mine house, and prove me now herewith, saith the LORD of hosts, if I will not open you the windows of heaven, and pour you out a blessing, that there shall not be room enough to receive it. And I will rebuke the devourer for your sakes, and he shall not destroy the fruits of your ground; neither shall your vine cast her fruit before the time in the field, saith the LORD of hosts"* (Malachi 3:10-11).

7. **Ensure that your Name is in the Book of Life in Heaven:** *"He that overcometh, the same shall be clothed in white raiment; and I will not blot out*

his name out of the book of life, but I will confess his name before my Father, and before his angels" (Revelation 3:5). *"And I saw the dead, small and great, stand before God; and the books were opened: and another book was opened, which is the book of life: and the dead were judged out of those things which were written in the books, according to their works"* (Revelation 20:12).

8. **Practise the Art of Praise and Worship in the Bathroom:** *"O clap your hands, all ye people; shout unto God with the voice of triumph… For God is the King of all the earth: sing ye praises with understanding. God reigneth over the heathen: God sitteth upon the throne of his holiness"* (Psalms 47:1, 7-8).

9. **Be Sensitive to the Promptings of the Spirit:** *"For as many as are led by the Spirit of God, they are the sons of God"* (Romans 8:14). *"This I say then, Walk in the Spirit, and ye shall not fulfil the lust of the flesh. For the flesh lusteth against the Spirit, and the Spirit against the flesh: and these are contrary the one to the other: so that ye cannot do the things that ye would. But if ye be led of the Spirit, ye are not under the law"* (Galatians 5:16-18).

Disobedience to the voice of the Lord and His commandments will always shut the heavens. *"But it shall come to pass, if thou wilt not hearken unto the voice of the LORD thy God, to observe to do all his commandments and his statutes which I command thee this day; that all these curses shall come upon thee, and overtake thee… And thy heaven that is over thy head shall be brass, and the earth that is under thee shall be iron. The LORD shall make the rain of thy land powder and dust: from heaven shall it come down upon thee, until thou be destroyed"* (Deuteronomy 28:15, 23-24).

9 | MULTI-DIMENSIONAL MINISTRY IN THE BATHROOM

09

Multi-Dimensional Ministry
in the Bathroom

"Follow the river and you will reach the sea" – **Ghanaian Proverb.**

The altar is a place of ministry. It is a place of service for those who are consecrated to serve as priests. The altar in the bathroom is particularly a place of multi-dimensional ministry. It is a place of:

1. Ministering to the Lord.

2. Ministering to yourself.

3. Ministering to your spouse and

4. Ministering to your children.

The multi-dimensional ministry in the bathroom should have the capacity for transforming individuals, families, institutions and nations. What happens in your bathroom should affect every aspect of your life.

MINISTERING TO THE LORD IN THE BATHROOM

Only those with Kingdom mind-sets can minister to the Lord. They seek first the Kingdom of God and His righteousness, trusting that all other things will be added to them. Their primary motivation is not what they will get, but what they can give. Such priests in the bathroom are selfless.

They seek a deeper dimension of intimacy with the Lord. They know the Lord's burdens and are not ashamed to carry them. Their heart's cry is: *"Lord let our hearts be broken by the things that break your heart."*

There is an erroneous thinking that ministering to the Lord is only about praise and worship. This is only an aspect of ministering to the Lord. Ministering to the Lord involves discovering His plans and purposes, the prophetic agenda for a given season and what He wants His people to do.

God dwells in eternity, but He rules over time. He has appointed specific times to accomplish certain purposes. Ministering to the Lord at the altar of your bathroom involves seeking God's face to discover what He wants His people to do. The restoration of the gospel of the Kingdom is a key focus for those who desire to minister to the Lord in this season.

The altar of the bathroom is a place to ask God vital and provoking questions of what you can do to advance the gospel of the Kingdom. What must you do to take over one of the seven mountains which oppose Gods' will? Which is the domain or mountain God wants you to take over? The prophetic words of Isaiah 2:1-4 cannot be fulfilled unless men and women are mobilised to take over the mountains that oppose God's will on earth. *"The word that Isaiah the son of Amoz saw concerning Judah and Jerusalem. And it shall come to pass in the last days, that the mountain of the LORD'S house shall be established in the top of the mountains, and shall be exalted above the hills; and all nations shall flow unto it. And many people shall go and say, Come ye, and let us go up to the mountain of the LORD, to the house of the God of Jacob; and he will teach us of his ways, and we will walk in his paths: for out of Zion shall go forth the law, and the word of the LORD from Jerusalem. And he shall judge among the nations, and shall rebuke many people: and they shall beat their swords into plowshares, and their spears into pruninghooks: nation shall not lift up sword against nation, neither shall they learn war any more."*

God is still asking, *"Whom will I send and who will go for us?"* Many are called but few are chosen, because only a few people can carry the burdens of the Lord. There is still a lot of ground to be conquered. The enemies of the Lord are still bestriding the seven mountains represented by the seven nations in Deuteronomy 7:1-4, *"When the LORD thy God shall bring thee into the land whither thou goest to possess it, and hath cast out many nations before thee, the Hittites, and the Girgashites, and the Amorites, and the Canaanites, and the Perizzites, and the Hivites, and the Jebusites, seven nations greater and mightier than thou; And when the LORD thy God shall deliver them before thee; thou shalt smite them, and utterly destroy them; thou shalt make no covenant with them, nor shew mercy unto them: Neither shalt thou make marriages with them; thy daughter thou shalt not give unto his son, nor his daughter shalt thou take unto thy son. For they will turn away thy son from following me that they may serve other gods: so will the anger of the LORD be kindled against you, and destroy thee suddenly."*

Ministering to the Lord in the bathroom will involve strategic level intercession to take over the seven mountains whose profiles are listed below.

JOHNNY ENLOW'S REVELATION FOR TAKING OVER THE SEVEN MOUNTAINS

S/N	Mountain	Enemy on the Mountain	Principality on the Mountain	Significant Displacing Authority	Basic Mission	Revelation 5:12 Key
1.	Media	Hittites *Represent Bad News*	Apollyon *Destroyer*	Evangelists	Fill the airwaves with "good news"	Blessing
2.	Government	Girgashites *Represent Corruption*	Lucifer *Pride And Manipulation*	Apostles	Fill government positions with humble servants, integrous leaders	Power
3.	Education	Amorites *Represent Humanism*	Beelzebub *Lies*	Teachers	Bring in new fear-of-God-based curriculum	Wisdom
4.	Economy	Canaanites *Represent Love Of Money*	Mammon *Greed*	Prophets	Discover and transfer wealth into Kingdom purposes	Riches
5.	Celebration	Hivites *Represent Compromise*	Jezebel *Seduction*	Prophets	Model the greater creative arts of God and prophesy through them	Glory
6.	Religion	Perizzites *Represent Idolatry*	The religious spirit *False Worship*	Holy Spirit	Model a Holy-Spirit-infused life and ministry	Honour
7.	Family	Jebusites *Represent Rejection*	Baal *Perversion*	Pastors	Impact social systems so that the family unit is prioritised	Strength

Johnny Enlow, *The Seven Mountain Prophecy*, pp.190-191

Don't be so concerned about what God must do for you. Take time to ask God what He would have you do for Him every day. Be willing to carry the burdens of the Lord. Develop a habit of asking God questions in the bathroom. Find out what you can help him do in your environment. This demands a sacrificial attitude, a selfless disposition.

As you minister to the Lord, carrying His burdens, God will increasingly give you direction. *"As they ministered to the Lord, and fasted, the Holy Ghost said, Separate me Barnabas and Saul for the work whereunto I have called them. And when they had fasted and prayed, and laid their hands on them, they sent them away. So they, being sent forth by the Holy Ghost, departed unto Seleucia; and from thence they sailed to Cyprus"* (Acts 13:2-4). Ministering to the Lord in your bathroom would mainly involve prayer, fasting, obeying His divine direction. It involves obeying the leadings of the Holy Spirit, doing what He wants you to do.

MINISTERING TO THE LESS PRIVILEGED AS AN ASPECT OF MINISTERING TO THE LORD

There are many helpless people around you. Carry their burdens in the place of intercession at the altar in your bathroom. Pray for them, ask God for divine insights into how you can physically minister to their needs. The Holy Spirit will put specific individuals in your heart to help. He will give you strategies for empowering them to help themselves. *"Pure religion and undefiled before God and the Father is this, to visit the fatherless and widows in their affliction, and to keep himself unspotted from the world"* (James 1:27).

Jesus taught that anyone who ministers to the hungry, the sick, the naked and the prisoner is vicariously ministering to Him. Such people will not be found in the bathroom, but we can ask God to guide us to help them at the point of ministering to the Lord in the bathroom. *"For I was an hungred, and ye gave me meat: I was thirsty, and ye gave me drink: I was a stranger, and ye took me in: Naked, and ye clothed me: I was sick, and ye visited me: I was in prison, and ye came unto me. Then shall the righteous answer him, saying, Lord, when saw we thee an hungred, and fed thee? or thirsty, and gave thee drink? When saw we thee a stranger, and took thee in? or naked, and clothed thee? Or when saw we thee sick, or in prison, and came unto thee? And the King shall answer and say unto them, Verily I say unto you, Inasmuch as ye have done it unto one of the least of these my brethren, ye have done it unto me"* (Matthew 25:35-40).

God is interested in food and agriculture policy. He is interested in health care delivery policy and several other policies listed below. Ministering to the needs of the poor is serving the Lord in practical and purposeful ways.

GOD'S INTEREST AND POLICY DESIGNS

S/N	Policy	Reference
1.	Food and Agriculture Policy.	*"I was hungry and you gave me food."*
2.	Water and Environmental Policy.	*"I was thirsty and you gave me drink."*
3.	Immigration and Emigration Policy.	*"I was a stranger and you took me in."*
4.	National Cover and Protection Policy.	*"I was naked and you clothed me."*
5.	Education and Information Policy.	*"I was thirsty and hungry for knowledge and you fed me."*
6.	Health Care Delivery Policy.	*"I was sick and you visited me."*
7.	Legal and Judicial Policy.	*"I was in prison and you came to me."*
8.	Policy of Substitutionary Sacrifice.	*"Then the righteous will answer Him, saying, 'Lord, when did we see You hungry and feed You...'"*

Pray for the grace to be an eye to the blind, feet to the lame and mouth to the dumb in the way Job was. *"Because I delivered the poor that cried, and the fatherless, and him that had none to help him. The blessing of him that was ready to perish came upon me: and I caused the widow's heart to sing for joy. I put on righteousness, and it clothed me: my judgment was as a robe and a diadem. I was eyes to the blind, and feet was I to the lame. I was a father to the poor: and the cause which I knew not I searched out. And I brake the jaws of the wicked, and plucked the spoil out of his teeth"* (Job 29:12-17).

10 | MINISTERING TO YOURSELF IN THE BATHROOM

10

Ministering to Yourself in the Bathroom

"If you wish to gather honey, you must be prepared to risk the painful sting of... bees" – **Nigerian Proverb.**

The bathroom is primarily a place of personal cleansing and purification. A revelation of the bathroom as an altar indicates that there is much more to what goes on there than mere personal purification.

Don't just clean your body in the bathroom. See every aspect of personal purification as a prophetic action with deep spiritual significance. Taking a bath should henceforth be seen as a spiritual venture. A few people would not begin to take their bath without spiritually sanctifying the water in the bath. Okechukwu O. Okechucku of the Africa Kingdom Business Forum, an arm of the Intercessors for Africa, has a tradition of blessing the water, the toothpaste and every other material required to clean his body. This is a clear example of ministering to one's self in the name of the Lord at the altar of the bathroom.

SANCTIFYING EVERY PART OF YOUR BODY

You too can see the process of cleaning your body as a prophetic action of seeking God's grace to spiritually clean every part of your body. As you wash your head, ask God to wash your mind by the water of His Word. As you clean your eyes, pray that the Lord will open your eyes and anoint them with eye-salve so you can see better in the realm of the spirit. As you clean your ears, tell God to remove every spiritual wax that hinders your ability to hear the voice of the Lord. As you wash your hands, tell God to

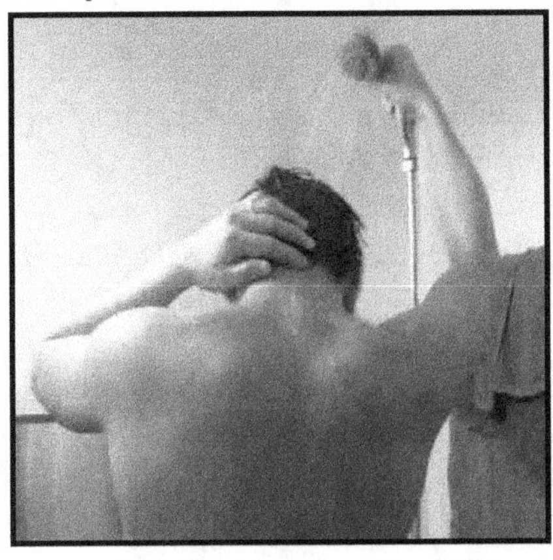

anoint them to prosper in whatever they find to do. As you clean your legs, declare that the steps of the righteous will be ordered by the Lord.

You could actually turn the whole process of taking a bath into a powerful tool of ministering to every part of your body with a view to activating them to function optimally. Remember that God's ministering angels who serve the heirs of salvation are always present around any body of consecrated water. The same is true of the Holy Spirit – who is ever ready to hover over water sanctified to deal with the problem of formlessness, emptiness and darkness. The presence of the Lord at the altar of your bathroom will ensure that the action of ministering to different parts of your body will not be in vain. God will always honour every act of faith based on the Word of God.

PERSONAL GATES TO BE SANCTIFIED AS YOU MINISTER TO YOURSELF IN THE BATHROOM

1. **Forehead:** *"And the LORD said unto him, Go through the midst of the city… and set a mark upon the foreheads of the men that sigh and that cry for all the abominations that be done in the midst thereof"* (Ezekiel 9:4). *"As an adamant harder than flint have I made thy forehead: fear them not, neither be dismayed at their looks, though they be a rebellious house"* (Ezekiel 3:9).

2. **Eyes:** *"Turn away mine eyes from beholding vanity; and quicken thou me in thy way"* (Psalm 119:37). *"And if thy right eye offend thee, pluck it out, and cast it from thee: for it is profitable for thee that one of thy members should perish, and not that thy whole body should be cast into hell"* (Matthew 5:29).

3. **Ears:** *"To whom shall I speak, and give warning, that they may hear? behold, their ear is uncircumcised, and they cannot hearken: behold, the word of the LORD is unto them a reproach; they have no delight in it"* (Jeremiah 6:10). *"He that hath an ear, let him hear what the Spirit saith unto the churches; To him that overcometh will I give to eat of the tree of life, which is in the midst of the paradise of God"* (Revelation 2:7).

4. **Nose:** *"Thus saith the Lord GOD… Behold, I will cause breath to enter into you, and ye shall live"* (Ezekiel 37:5). *"All the while my breath is in me, and the Spirit of God is in my nostrils"* (Job 27:3)

5. **Hands:** *"If I wash myself with snow water, and make my hands never so clean; Yet shalt thou plunge me in the ditch, and mine own clothes shall abhor me"* (Job 9:30-31). *"Whatsoever thy hand findeth to do, do it with thy might; for there is no work, nor device, nor knowledge, nor wisdom, in the grave, whither thou goest"* (Ecclesiastes 9:10).

6. **Feet:** *"He maketh my feet like hinds' feet, and setteth me upon my high places"* (Psalms 18:33). *"…thou hast set my feet in a large room"* (Psalms 31:8). *"And your feet shod with the preparation of the gospel of peace"* (Ephesians 6:15).

7. **Heart:** *"And I will give them one heart, and I will put a new spirit within you; and I will take the stony heart out of their flesh, and will give them an heart of flesh"* (Ezekiel 11:19). *"And I will give them an heart to know me, that I am the LORD: and they shall be my people, and I will be their God: for they shall return unto me with their whole heart"* (Jeremiah 24:7).

8. **Armpits:** *"And the LORD said furthermore unto him, Put now thine hand into thy bosom. And he put his hand into his bosom: and when he took it out, behold, his hand was leprous as snow. And he said, Put thine hand into thy bosom again. And he put his hand into his bosom again; and plucked it out of his bosom, and, behold, it was turned again as his other flesh"* (Exodus 4:6-7).

9. **Finger:** *"Then shalt thou call, and the LORD shall answer; thou shalt cry, and he shall say, Here I am. If thou take away from the midst of thee the yoke, the putting forth of the finger, and speaking vanity"* (Isaiah 58:9). *"But if I with the finger of God cast out devils, no doubt the kingdom of God is come upon you"* (Luke 11:20).

10. **Sex Organs:** *"…Now the body is not for fornication, but for the Lord; and the Lord for the body… Flee fornication. Every sin that a man doeth is without the body; but he that committeth fornication sinneth against his own body. What? know ye not that your body is the temple of the Holy Ghost which is in you, which ye have of God, and ye are not your own? For ye are bought with a price: therefore glorify God in your body, and in your spirit, which are God's"* (1 Corinthians 6:13, 18-20).

11. **Mouth and Tongue:** *"My lips shall not speak wickedness, nor my tongue utter deceit"* (Job 27:4). *"Then flew one of the seraphims unto me, having a live coal in his hand, which he had taken with the tongs from off the altar: And he laid it upon my mouth, and said, Lo, this hath touched thy lips; and thine iniquity is taken away, and thy sin purged"* (Isaiah 6:6-7). *"Even so the tongue is a little member, and boasteth great things. Behold, how great a matter a little fire kindleth!"* (James 3:5). *"The Spirit of the LORD spake by me, and his word was in my tongue"* (2 Samuel 23:2). (Source: Ogan Steve, The Prophetic Significance of 2011, pp.439-440).

Every part of your body is a gateway. Prophetically sanctifying your body in the way described above will establish them as gateways of righteousness. The altar of your body will be linked to the Lamb's altar in Heaven as you undertake this prophetic action.

11
MINISTERING TO YOUR
SPOUSE IN THE BATHROOM

11

Ministering to Your Spouse in the Bathroom

"Those who sow thorns should not expect to reap flowers" – **Swazi Proverb.**

Couples can turn the bathroom into a powerful place of mutual ministration. This will require a willingness of those who are legally married to take their baths together. Traditional and conservative couples always find this difficult to do. But there is really nothing wrong with husbands and wives taking their bath together and using this opportunity to minister to the Lord together and to each other. Adam and Eve were naked before each other. *"And they were both naked, the man and his wife, and were not ashamed"* (Genesis 2:25). They often took their bath together at the river that had its source from Eden which parted into four heads

FOUR RIVER HEADS IN WHICH ADAM AND EVE BATHED TOGETHER

Given our current understanding that consecrated water bodies are the habitation of the Holy Spirit and Angels, the prophetic significance of the four rivers in which Adam and Eve took their bath together become significant. *"And a river went out of Eden to water the garden; and from thence it was parted, and became into four heads. The name of the first is Pison: that is it which compasseth the whole land of Havilah, where there is gold; And the gold of that land is good: there is bdellium and the onyx stone. And the name of the second river is Gihon: the same is it that compasseth the whole land of Ethiopia. And the name of the third river is Hiddekel: that is it which goeth toward the east of Assyria. And the fourth river is Euphrates"* (Genesis 2:10-14).

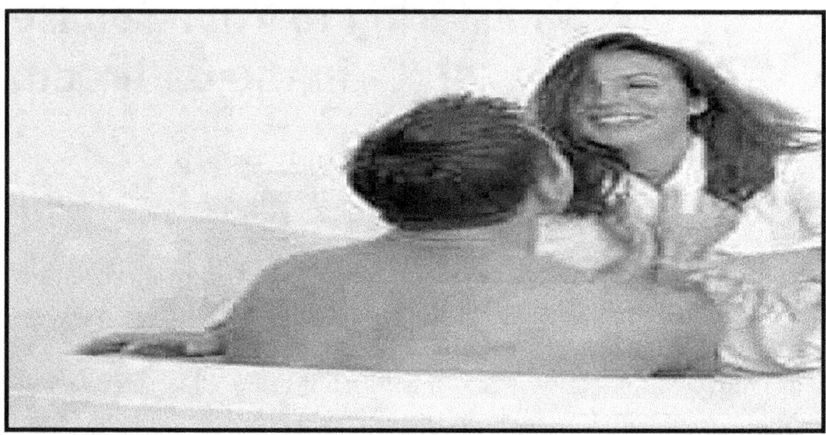

The fact that Adam and Eve were naked before each other and were not ashamed gives us an indication that they were willing to mutually minister to each other without reservation. The character of the rivers obviously influenced their ministry to each other.

1. **Pison:** This is the first river which skirted around the whole land of Havilah. It symbolised *"free flowing"* grace. Bathing in this river and ministering to each other at its bank was a means of invoking the spirit of freedom and liberty.

2. **Gihon:** The second river which compassed the land of Cush means *"busting forth"*. It was a source of energy and vigour.

3. **Hiddekel:** The third river, which is also called Tigris, flowed east of Assyria and means *"rapid result"*. It was a source of overcoming delay.

4. **Euphrates:** The fourth and final river, which means *"that which makes fruitful"*, was a means of invoking greater productivity.

Adam and Eve drank from these springs. About 70% of their bodies were constituted by water. Like our spiritual parents, we too have the heritage of these springs. In fact, God in Psalm 87:6 says that *"… All my springs are in you"*. This simply means that Pison, Gihon, Hiddekel and Euphrates are in us. Remember that 70% of the human body is made up of water.

MINISTERING TO YOUR SPOUSE BY ACTIVATING THE SPRINGS WITHIN

Every husband and wife has a part of the four river heads that came out of Eden in them. To effectively minister to your spouse at the altar in the bathroom, activate these springs for the purpose of purifying your partner. Declare freedom from bondage for your spouse based on the spring of Pison. Call forth the river of energy and vigour from the fountains of the

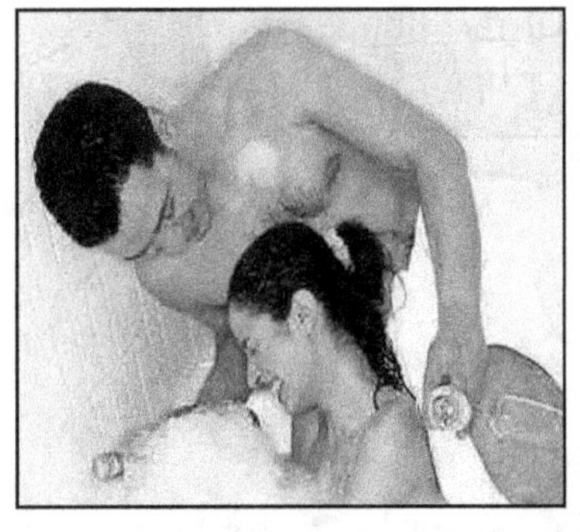

Gihon in you. Let it restore lost energy and revive waning strength. Invoke the river of rapid result to help your spouse overcome delays. Make a rainbow proclamation on each other based on Revelation 10:1, 6, *"And I saw another mighty angel come down from heaven, clothed with a cloud: and a rainbow was upon his head, and his face was as it were the sun, and his feet as pillars of fire… And sware by him that liveth forever and ever, who created heaven, and the things that therein are, and the earth, and the things that therein are, and the sea, and the things which are therein, that there should be delay no longer."* Activate the river of "that which makes fruitful" in each other. The spring of fruitfulness is already in both of you. Ask the Holy Spirit to stir up everything in your relationship that has the capacity to enhance fruitfulness.

If God's Word says that all God's springs are in us, it means that a reasonable quantity of the 70% of the water content in our body has its source flowing from the four rivers of Eden. Husbands can wash off every contamination of these springs in their wives. They can call forth the swift restoration of Pison, Gihon, Hiddekel and Euphrates in their wives. Similarly, wives can also scrub off spiritual pollutants that hinder their husbands from manifesting the prophetic character of the springs in them, for the purpose of ensuring freedom, rapid results, and exceeding fruitfulness.

For many couples, bathing together is merely a prelude to enjoying intimate sexual relationships in the bathroom. There is nothing wrong with enjoying sexual fulfilment at the altar in the bathroom. Nevertheless, since marriage is a ministry and couples are on assignment, to restrict ministering to your spouse in the bathroom to sex is to elevate the sensual above the spiritual. This will be unfortunate notwithstanding the fact that couples have all the right to enjoy intimacy in the bathroom.

12
MINISTERING TO YOUR
CHILDREN IN THE BATHROOM

12

Ministering to Your Children in the Bathroom

Children are God's heritage and parents are essentially care-takers. God expects parents to help children to discover the redemptive gifts embedded in them. He has given parents the mandate to help children to harness and develop their talents with a view to deploying them to fulfil God's plans and purposes for nations.

The process of accomplishing these awesome parental functions is tasking. This probably explains why someone once said that the *"most difficult job on earth is not being a president but being a parent."* Ministering to your children is not just physically and emotionally demanding, it is spiritually sapping but ultimately eternally rewarding. To see a child become all that God created him to be is a joy to behold. This explains why Psalm 127: 4-5 says, *"As arrows in the hand of a mighty one, so are the sons of the young men. O the happiness of the man who hath filled his quiver with them, they are not ashamed, for they speak with enemies in the gate!"*

Parents should harness every opportunity to minister to their children. One of the best times to make eternal investments into a child is at bath time. Every child should be given a bath at least two times every day. Bath time is not only a moment of cleaning up a child. It is also a time of bonding between parents and children. More importantly, it can even be a time of unceasing intercession and instruction for a child. It can be a time of moulding the destiny of children, and by extension of nations.

PREPARING TO GIVE YOUR BABY A BATH

It has been said that prayerful preparation prevents bad performance. Again, those who fail to prepare have prepared to fail. "For *Ezra had prepared his heart to seek the law of the Lord, and to do it, and to teach statutes and ordinances in Israel*" (Ezra 7:10).

In like manner, parents must prepare to make spiritual investments in their children at bath time. The task of giving your children a bath should not be permanently contracted to maids or nannies. You may of course allow them to assist you once in a while, but no parent should totally hand over

the task of giving his or her children a bath to "strangers". Bath time is bonding time. Bath time is instruction time. Bath time is a spiritual and strategic time for laying the foundations of a child's future.

Prepare to give your child a bath both physically and spiritually. Ensure that all you need are available before you begin the task. Create a special bathroom atmosphere for your child with powerful pictures and intelligently crafted instructional materials. Sanctify your baby's bathroom and raise an altar there. Speak to the child as you give him or her a bath. Let bath time be Bible study time. Let bath time be a time of praise and worship.

PROPHESYING TO YOUR CHILDREN AT BATH TIME

Ask the Holy Spirit for divine direction for every bath time. Be creative and innovative to make bath time interesting and unforgettable. Prophesy to your baby at bath time. Proclaim the sure word of prophecy as you clean specific portions of your baby's body. Tell God to anoint your baby's eyes with eye-salve as you wash these vital organs of his or her body. Dedicate and rededicate the reproductive gates. Declare that they shall not be polluted, defiled or misused. Use bath time to prophesy that the spirit that

works in the children of disobedience will not work in your children. Declare that you and the children God has given to you are for signs and wonders. Pray for your children that they will grow up to fulfil God's purposes.

Every child is an arrow in a hand of a mighty man. "*As arrows in the hand of a mighty one So are the sons of the young men*" (Psalm 127:4). An arrow is a weapon of war. It must be sharpened, positioned in a bow, and drawn close to the heart of the one appointed to release it on target. Use bath times to seek God's revelation as to what type of arrow your child has been sharpened to be. Be sensitive to discover the destiny of the child at the altar of the bathroom through the invocation of the spirit's presence. Draw the child close to you and ultimately to his Maker. Position the children in the divine bow that will eventually enable him or her to be released on target. Find out what the proper target of a child is, what he or she was created to do and ensure that the child is on target by the time he matures to give himself a bath.

HOW JECOBED MINISTERED TO MOSES AT BATH TIME

Moses was born at a time of crisis. His mother recognized the prophetic mandate of his life and was determined to preserve him, although Pharaoh decreed that every Hebrew male-child must be killed. Jecobed kept Moses for three months. *"But when she could no longer hide him, she took an ark of bulrushes for him daubet it with asphalt and pitch put the child in it and laid it in the reeds by the river's bank"* (Exodus 2:3). Miriam, his sister, watched to see what would become of him. Heaven must have dispatched the angels of the waters to guide the ark that carried Israel's future deliverer to the place where he could be rescued.

The story of how Moses was rescued is told in Exodus 2:4 – 10. *"His sister stood at a distance to see what would happen to him. Then Pharaoh's daughter went down to the Nile to bathe, and her attendants were walking along the riverbank. She saw the basket among the reeds and sent her female slave to get it. She opened it and saw the baby. He was crying, and she felt sorry for him. "This is one of the Hebrew babies," she said. Then his sister asked Pharaoh's daughter, "Shall I go and get one of the Hebrew women to nurse the baby for you?" "Yes, go," she answered. So the girl went and got the baby's mother. Pharaoh's daughter said to her, "Take this baby and nurse him for me, and I will pay you." So the woman took the baby and nursed him. When the child grew older, she took him to Pharaoh's daughter and he became her son. She named him Moses, saying, "I drew him out of the water"* (Exodus 2:4–10).

Moses was an Egyptian by naturalisation but a Hebrew at heart. Why? Because at bath time and every other opportunity, his mother kept on instructing him about his real identity. Jecobed told Moses that he was a "beautiful child" appointed to deliver the children of Israel from bondage.

She instructed him about God's prophecy that the Jews will be delivered from bondage after 400 years. She prepared him to play his prophetic role.

Pharaoh's daughter called her adopted son Moses *"because I drew him out of the waters"*. Moses' biological mother used water at bath time to symbolically draw his attention to the water of God's Word and his prophetic mandate as a deliverer. Moses himself did a lot of ministry on water, dividing the Red Sea for the children of Israel to cross over, healing the bitter waters of Marah, providing water at Meribah when the congregation needed it and breaking the heads of the sea serpents and water spirits in the process of engaging in aquatic warfare as Psalm 74:13-14 indicates: *"It was you who split open the sea by your power; you broke the heads of the monster in the waters. It was you who crushed the heads of Leviathan and gave it as food to the creatures of the desert."*

There is no doubt that God used bath time to prepare Moses to fulfil his mandate especially in the context of dealing with water spirits. The faith of Jecobed was transferred into Moses at bath time when he was still very young. No wonder Moses himself became a great man of faith according to Hebrews 11:23-29, *"By faith Moses' parents hid him for three months after he was born, because they saw he was no ordinary child, and they were not afraid of the king's edict. By faith Moses, when he had grown up, refused to be known as the son of Pharaoh's daughter. He chose to be mistreated along with the people of God rather than to enjoy the fleeting pleasures of sin. He regarded disgrace for the sake of Christ as of greater value than the treasures of Egypt, because he was looking ahead to his reward. By faith he left Egypt, not fearing the king's anger; he persevered because he saw him who is invisible. By faith he kept the Passover and the application of blood, so that the destroyer of the firstborn would not touch the firstborn of Israel. By faith the people passed through the Red Sea as on dry land; but when the Egyptians tried to do so, they were drowned."*

Bath time is a time to raise men and women of faith. Bath time is a time to raise deliverers who will guide nations into their promised land. Bath time is a time of cleansing, purifying and sanctifying potential leaders.

PROPHETIC PROCLAMATION TO MAKE WHILE GIVING YOUR CHILD A BATH

"Jane is a heritage of the Lord, the fruit of my womb that will bring many generations a reward. You are an arrow in the hand of the mighty man, a weapon of war that cannot be defeated. The spirit that works in the children of disobedience will not work in you. The corruption that perverts agents of redemption will not pervert your destiny. You are not of them who, in the last days, will be lovers of themselves, lovers of money, boasters, proud, blasphemers, disobedient to parents, unthankful, unholy, unloving, unforgiving, slanderers, without self-control, brutal, despisers of good, traitors, headstrong, haughty, lovers of pleasure rather than lovers of God.

Jane is a lover of God, humble, obedient, thankful, holy, forgiving and truthful. You are self-controlled, dependable, loyal and sacrificial. You shall be taught of the Lord and great shall be your peace. Your steps shall be ordered by the Lord. The favour of the Lord shall follow you. The Lord is your judge. The Lord is your lawgiver. The Lord is your King. He will save you."

13

AVOIDING DEATH IN A
PLACE OF LIFE

13

Avoiding Death in a Place of Life

*"If a fish refuses to open its mouth, it doesn't
get caught"* – **Togolese Proverb.**

Altars are centres for enacting and sustaining the covenant of life and peace. Unfortunately, the enemy seeks to pervert their identity by orchestrating incidents contrary to their original purpose. The principle that explains Satan's perversion of God's creations is John 10:10: *"The thief comes only to steal and kill and destroy; I have come that they may have life, and have it to the full."*

Although the altar in the bathroom is a place of purification, sanctification and restoration of life, people have had unhealthy experiences there. The altar of life has witnessed the death of countless number of people. Some people have lost their lives in the bathroom not because it is God's will for them to die there. Others have been badly injured because Satan set a trap in the bathroom to cut their lives short or to hinder their fulfilment of destiny. *Joni Erickson Tada* was maimed in a swimming pool accident. She has, however, excelled in her chosen profession notwithstanding the terrible injury she sustained. She became a wheelchair-ridden quadriplegic.

Dedicate the bathroom and every gadget in it. Be careful that electricity in the bathroom is properly wired. Water can activate a naked wire and cause electrocution. Francois C. Tande, a French Pop singer in the 1960s, had an obsession with cleanliness. *"He was electrocuted in the bathroom of his Paris apartment as he tried to fix a broken light bulb while standing in a water-filled bathtub."* A friend's daughter, wonderful and intelligent, was also electrocuted in the bathroom. She was a trailblazer who at 13 years acted like a mature and intelligent woman. She was so intelligent that virtually every known award for her peers in school and in church was given to her. She was a straight A student academically. She was very well behaved, diligent and the pride of her parents. Unfortunately she died in the place of life.

Sanctify your bathroom physically and spiritually. Ensure that it is always clean. Bring the cover of the Holy Spirit and angelic forces into your bathroom. This is important given the fact that Satan seeks to counterfeit every aspect of God's creation. Just as the Holy Spirit and angels are often seen in association with altars and water bodies, so also Satan and his fallen angels love to hang around water bodies and bathrooms. There are specific bathrooms they have access to because they have been dedicated as satanic altars. Consequently, while some bathrooms are altars of life and peace, others are altars of death and hell. The character of a bathroom is determined by the type of altar raised there.

The bathroom of those involved in occultism or Satanism will obviously be altars of death. Nevertheless, even altars raised unto God can be polluted and perverted if the priests who should safeguard and sustain ministry there are careless or lukewarm. The parable of the wheat and the tares shows that it was while men slept that the enemy sowed tares in a field that was originally meant for wheat.

The parents of the 13-year-old girl who was electrocuted in the bathroom are Christians. Someone close to them actually dreamt about the incident, but could not reach to warn them until after the tragedy happened. This is unfortunate. But it should serve as a lesson to quicken parents to be more sensitive about the circumstances around their home.

Invoke the presence of God's angels in your bathroom. Cultivate the habit of praising God at this altar of sanctification. God inhabits the praises of his people and will always be present in the bathroom even when your children are taking their baths alone. Be safety conscious in your home. Do not allow the children to lock the bathroom like adults when they are there alone. Make provision for an alarm to contact people outside the bathroom in an emergency. One woman stayed in the bathroom for three weeks because the door was jammed. Every effort to get attention by banging the door failed until one

neighbour eventually responded and called the police for help. This woman mysteriously survived by taking constant baths which brought her regular refreshment. She also kept herself alive by drinking a lot of water.

KINGS WHO DIED IN THE BATHROOM

1. **Emperor Heliogabalus of Rome, 204 – 222:** This was an eccentric, idolatrous and abominable personality. He practiced homosexuality and worshipped Baal, the Syrian god. He was killed with his mother in the bathroom after he ran there for safety. Their heads were cut off and their bodies thrown into a river in Tiber.

2. **King Edward the Second of England, 980 – 1016:** He went to the bathroom to "answer the call of nature" and was stabbed to death there from beneath.

3. **King James the Third of Scotland, 1394 – 1437:** He was killed in a small toilet at Perth Abbey where he ran to hide from assassins. They broke the door to the toilet and stabbed him in the chest sixteen times with swords and daggers.

4. **King Henry the Third of France, 1555 – 1589:** He also went to the toilet to answer the call of nature and was stabbed just as he was leaving the toilet by a Jacobin priest. Although the priest who killed King Henry III was also killed, *"his corpse was put on trial for the assassination."*

5. **King George the Second of Great Britain and Ireland, 1683 – 1760:** He died in the bathroom after having a breakfast of hot chocolate. He was discovered there by his German valet who heard him fall and later found the king on the bathroom floor. King George cut his face as he fell on the ground.

The death of these kings in the bathroom exemplified judgments for many abominable practices. Take the case of Emperor Heliogabalus of 3rd century Rome, also known as Elagabalus. He lived a scandalous life, marrying five women and divorcing all five. One of those Elagabalus married was a Vestal virgin (a holy priestess) who under Roman law should have been buried alive for losing her virginity. He was murdered in the bathroom with his mother by his grandmother and aunt who were appalled by the fact that the Emperor was a bisexual.

FAMOUS PEOPLE IN CONTEMPORARY TIMES WHO DIED IN THE BATHROOM

Bathroom fatalities are not restricted to ancient kings. Several famous people in the recent past have also died in the bathroom. Some contemporary cases of deaths in the bathroom were undoubtedly cases of judgments against celebrities who lived perverted lifestyles.

1. **Judy Garland, 1922 – 1996:** She was an American singer and actress. She died of drug overdose in the bathroom of her London home.

2. **Elvis Presley, 1935 – 1977:** Regarded as a king of Rock and Roll, Elvis died of a heart attack at his Graceland home in Memphis. He was, however, known to have been addicted to prescription drugs and lived a rough lifestyle.

3. **Lenny Bruce, 1925 – 1966:** He used foul language at a time when such profanity was rare. He was addicted to drugs and *"was found dead in the bathroom of his Hollywood Hills home with a syringe, a burned bottle cap, and other drug paraphernalia."* The official cause of death *"was acute morphine poisoning caused by an accidental overdose."*

4. **Jim Morrison, 1943 – 1971:** He was a musician, the lead singer of a Rock band called *The Doors*. Morrison died in his bathtub in Paris. He was notorious for drugs and alcohol abuse, which obviously aided his death. (http://blog.funstylers.com/uncategorised/bathroom).

Notice that all the people mentioned above were musicians and comedians who lived a riotous life of alcohol and drug abuse. Why they died in the bathroom, a place associated with restoration and revival, tells us that an altar of life and peace can also be a place of death and hell for those who live perverted lifestyles.

14 | THE BEAUTY OF THE BATHROOM

14

The Beauty of the Bathroom

"Truth is like oil, no matter how much water you pour on it, it will always float" – **Nigerian Proverb.**

Notwithstanding the deaths associated with bathrooms, this altar is a place of beauty and breakthroughs for those who walk in the Spirit. The beauty of the bathroom is first and foremost spiritual. But it must also be aesthetic.

Many people don't want to enter their bathroom unless it is absolutely necessary. This is because these bathrooms are ordinary rather than extraordinary. Some bathrooms repel rather than attract you. But the bathroom should be spiritually and physically magnetic. This is possible if you invoke the presence of the Holy Spirit and make an effort to modernise and beautify your bathroom. I personally do not like the way my bathroom is currently. I am praying and believing God for the resources to bring it to the level where its physical outlook will match the spiritual investment made there.

HOW TO BEAUTIFY YOUR BATHROOM

Get a creative architect to design a befitting and beautiful bathroom concept when you are building a new house or remodelling the old. Make provisions for a Jacuzzi or any of the creative bathtubs in the market. Don't be extravagant, but feel free to transform this vital segment of your home without feeling guilty. After all, your motive for beautifying your bathroom is because it is an altar raised unto the Lord.

Get a music player with spiritual songs in your bathroom. Ensure that you also have the Bible on CD. Make adequate room in the bathroom. Ensure that the technology in your bathroom is up to date. DVICE, a business outfit that specialises on home gadgets, recently showcased creative and awesome gadgets for the bathroom. Prefacing their advert were these words: *"Oh, the bathroom! What a delightful little room. And whether it's your sanctuary or just a place to do your business, we at DVICE think this calls for celebration..."* Yes indeed! The revelation of the prophetic significance of the bathroom and why it must be a place of beauty calls for celebration.

BEAUTIFUL GADGETS FOR THE BATHROOM

Some of awesome gadgets advertised by DVICE include:

1. **Planetarium Bath Light:** This gadget showcases lighting systems that *"switch between Rose Bath and Deep Ocean Water graphics to change your mood."* Its essence is to help you *"relax after a long day at work."* The Planetarium bath light is designed to be waterproof and *"floats in the tubs while projecting images of stars all over your wall."* It will help you to appreciate the wonders of God's creation as you worship the Creator at the altar in your bathroom. Redeem whatever planetarium bath light you buy to be sure it was not dedicated to waters spirits or made for occultic purposes.

2. **Whirlpool Tub:** The sales people at DVICE say that *"when no other bath will do, this one has it all: massage jets, hydro jets, and chromo therapy systems."* The whirlpool tub has *"512 different colour choices to create the most calming, custom bath experience ever."*

3. **Alsons Showerheads:** These are crafted by Alsons, a company that specialises in bathroom technology. Unlike most showers that have about 40 or less spray holes, Alsons showerhead *"has a whopping 158 spray holes..."* They enable the shower to run with generous abandon unlike the showerhead that hoards water as though there is a water recession.

4. **Robot Toilet Paper Holder:** This is an improvement on the toilet papers that hang on the wall, which are often inaccessible. All you need to do to get your toilet paper is to *"turn the knob on the side and, voilà! Toilet paper!"* The toilet papers in the Robot Toilet Paper Holder come in different creative colours.

5. **Wall-Mounted Toothpaste Squeezer:** DVICE says that *"for those of us who have fought and lost against those stubborn toothpaste tubes, the struggle is over. This simple little gadget makes sure every last bit of toothpaste gets out of the tube and unto your toothbrush where they belong."*

6. **Aqua-Notes:** For writers and many who receive inspirations in the bathroom, this is a miracle gadget. Aqua-Notes are *"waterproof notepads for a more productive bath time."* The divine insights received at the altar of revelation in the bathroom will no longer be forgotten and lost because there is nowhere to write them. (http://dvice.com/archives/2010)

HYDROTHERAPY AND THE HEALING VIRTUES OF TAKING A BATH

Taking a bath is not always a matter of "getting clean". It is sometimes a therapeutic desire to unwind in order to be emotionally, psychologically or even physically healed of stress and others ailments. Hydrotherapy is the use of water or the act of taking a bath as a restorative process. It has been said that *"baths have many healing powers – from a sitz bath for haemorrhoids to soaks that relieve pain or itching."* The benefits of hydrotherapy include:

1. **Solution to Skin Problems:** A bath can be used to treat poison ivy, hives, dry skin, inflamed skin and itching.

2. **Easing of Labour Pains during Childbirth:** A woman in labour can experience reduction in her labour pains by taking a strategic bath. Furthermore, *"a bath may be part of episiotomy care."*

3. **Lowering of Pulse and Body Temperature:** A bath can also help to decrease one's body temperature as well as an irregular pulse.

4. **Easing of Muscle Spasms and Healing of Haemorrhoids:** A warm bath is a therapeutic means of easing muscle spasms and healing "rectal problems" and haemorrhoids.

5. **Reducing the Pain of Arthritis and Menstrual Cramps:** Those suffering from arthritis can get relative relief by merely sitting in water. Water is also a means of easing menstrual cramps.

6. **Dealing with Emotional Tension and Anxiety:** Those suffering from tensions, anxieties and emotional instabilities can get needed relief if they take a warm and soothing bath. This will aid the ability to relax more and sleep better.

7. **Healing of Rashes, Insect Bites and Eczema:** This can be achieved through the therapeutic effect of salt baths. Salt in water with the right medical attention can bring healing to anyone suffering from rashes, insect bites and eczema.

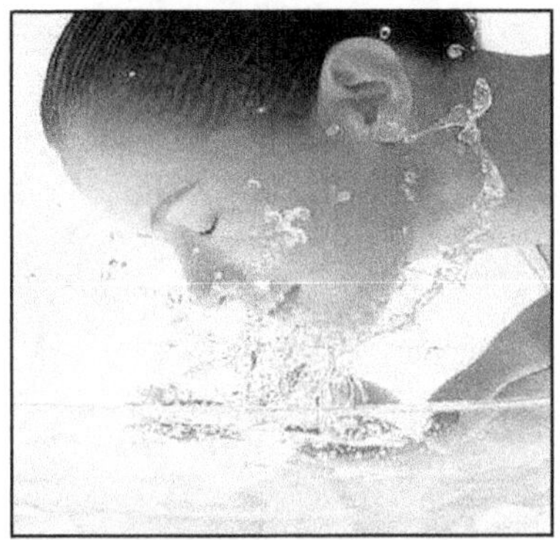

The scent of water in a consecrated bathroom is beautiful. It relaxes tired nerves, aids emotional restoration and helps those who have difficulty sleeping. Nevertheless, everyone must be safety-conscious in the bathroom. Consult your doctor to be sure that a particular aspect of hydrotherapy is compatible with your health needs. Don't stay in the bath for too long. Ensure that you don't sleep off in the bathtub, as this can cause drowning. Use water that is warm, tepid or cool. Avoid the use of water that is unclean or too hot as this can damage your skin. Keep a bath mat in the bathtub and on the floor to avoid slipping and falling. Ensure that your towels are clean and comfortable.

Your bathroom should give glory to God. It is an altar of revelation, restoration and sanctification. It is a spiritual highway that should link your home with the River of Life and the Lamb's altar in Heaven. Remember that fruitfulness, deliverance and divine health all proceed from the River of Life for the healing of individuals, the transformation of nations and restoration of divine intimacy with the Lord. *"And he shewed me a pure river of water of life, clear as crystal, proceeding out of the throne of God and of the Lamb. In the midst of the street of it, and on either side of the river, was there the tree of life, which bare twelve manners of fruits, and yielded her fruit every month: and the leaves of the tree were for the healing of the nations. And there shall be no more curse: but the throne of God and of the Lamb shall be in it; and his servants shall serve him: And they shall see his face; and his name shall be in their foreheads"* (Revelation 22:1-4).

15 | THE BEAUTY AND BLACK SIDE OF BATHROOM POETRY

15

The Beauty and Black Side
of Bathroom Poetry

"You do not consult an oracle when you already know the cause of your illness" – **Cameroonian Proverb.**

There is an overflowing stream of poetic unction in the bathroom. This explains why many wordsmiths have been productive in the bathroom. Poems have been crafted; songs have been written and the bathroom continues to activate the powerful pens of ready writers. It is unfortunate, however, that bathroom poetry has been used to mess up the walls of public and private bathrooms. One anonymous poet had this to say about writing poems on the walls of bathrooms.

Those who write on bathroom walls
Roll their shit in little balls
And those who read these words of wit
Eat these little balls of shit.

This poet seemed to have been complaining of messing up bathroom walls with poems. Ironically, his piece of critical poetry in foul language was also written on a bathroom wall. Another poet complained about the unhealthy habit of stealing toilet paper from public toilets.

Here I lie in stinky vapour
Because some bastard stole the toilet paper,
Shall I lie, or shall I linger,
Or shall I be forced to use my finger.

Here I sit,
Broken-hearted.
Tried to shit,
But only farted.

Thank God that this bathroom poet did not have to use his finger in the place of toilet paper. He was so broken-hearted by the fact that someone stole the toilet paper that he "only farted" when he "tried to shit." All things seemed to have worked together for his good eventually.

The bathroom is indeed a beautiful place of creativity. It affords people an opportunity to express themselves in writing. One writer who was bent on stopping the unhealthy practice of putting cigarette butts in toilet bowls wrote thus: *"Please do not throw cigarette butts in our urinal. We don't piss in your ashtrays!"*

Good advice! Those who clog the toilet bowls with their cigarette butts should be warned because if they don't stop their wicked habits, they may one day find that someone they have offended may urinate in their ashtrays.

People have personal reasons for using the public toilet. Some go to ease themselves. Others go for other reasons. One lover of bathroom poetry had this to say about the different reasons people visit the bathroom:

Some come here to sit and think,
Some come here to shit and stink,
But I come here to scratch my balls,
And to read the bullshit on the walls.

As humorous as these bathroom poems may seem, their contents are not always edifying. Whatever is done in the bathroom must conform to the standards of righteousness. Every altar, whether in public places or private homes, must be kept holy. Don't yield to the temptation of defiling

a place sanctified for glorifying God. Some people go into the toilet to practise the despicable act of masturbation. Others are lured to steal toilet paper meant for everyone to use. It has been noted that 79% of Americans who use public toilets steal the toilet paper there. No wonder one of our bathroom poets complained of lying in *"stinky vapour, because some bastard stole the toilet paper."*

Go into the bathroom with great expectation. Your creative instincts will be quickened and awakened by the Holy Spirit. Be ready to receive bestselling book ideas. Be open to receive divine insights from above. There is a deep unction that will call forth the deep in you.

When the deep bubbles
And the waters are heated to boil
There is a steam that rises
To give men wings to fly

When the heavens receive incense from the earth
And the mystery of union conceives a new agenda
There is a rain of glory that falls
On men to quicken the dead

When minds are sharpened by the sword of the Spirit
And the dull are quickened and awakened by fire
There is a new cutting edge that
Breaks the barriers of limitation

When the plans in time align with
The programmes in eternity
And Divinity restores Humanity
There is a new song heard in heaven and on earth

So let the deep bubble
Let the waters be heated to boil
A steam will rise to give you
Wings to fly.

Let the heavens receive incense from the earth
Let the mystery of union conceive a new agenda
A rain of glory will fall
To quicken even the dead

Let the mind be sharpened by the sword of the Spirit
Let the dull be quickened and awakened by fire
A new cutting edge will
Break the barriers of your limitations

Let the plans in time align with
The programmes in eternity
Let Divinity restore Humanity
A new song will be heard in heaven and on earth

When the deep bubbles
And the waters are heated to boil
There is a steam that rises
To give men wings to fly

The deep will bubble as you wait on the Lord in the bathroom. The waters in you will be heated to boil and a divine steam will rise to give you fresh wings to fly.

16 | BATHING AND PRAYING IN THE BATHROOM AT THE HOURS OF PRAYER

16

Bathing and Praying in the Bathroom at the Hours of Prayer

"If the right hand washes the left hand and the left hand washes the right hand, both hands will be clean" – **Lesotho Proverb**

There are no universally stimulated and acceptable bath times. Most people generally tend to take their bath early in the morning in preparation to go to work and late at night in readiness to retire to sleep. Others take their bath in-between the morning and night times, depending on how they feel. Bath time is, therefore, dependent on individual needs, engagements and desires.

Nevertheless, a fresh revelation of the prophetic significance of the bathroom and bathing should motivate us to take strategic baths based on the biblical revelation of the hours of prayer and what each hour represents in terms of the content of prayer to be rendered. Apart from taking our baths according to the hours of prayer, we could also do so based on the structure of biblical watches.

WATCHES OF THE DAY

Watches	Durations
First Watch	6:00 a.m. – 9:00 a.m.
Second Watch	9:00 a.m. – 12:00 noon
Third Watch	12:00 noon – 3:00 p.m.
Fourth Watch	3:00 p.m. – 6:00 p.m.

WATCHES OF THE NIGHT

Watches	Durations
First Watch	6:00 p.m. – 9:00 p.m.
Second Watch	9:00 p.m. – 12:00 midnight
Third Watch	12:00 midnight – 3:00 a.m.
Fourth Watch	3:00 a.m. – 6:00 a.m.

Each of the watches begin with an hour of prayer. Again the suggestion that strategic baths should be taken based on the hours of prayer should not be taken rigidly. It should not be turned into a doctrine which must be obeyed. Only strategic baths, designed to accomplish specific purposes should be tied to the hours of prayer relevant to the purpose to be achieved.

THE HOURS OF PRAYER

S/N	Hours	Time of the Day
1.	First Hour of Prayer	6:00 a.m.
2.	Third Hour of Prayer	9:00 a.m.
3.	Sixth Hour of Prayer	12:00 noon
4.	Ninth Hour of Prayer	3:00 p.m.
5.	Twelfth Hour of Prayer	6:00 p.m.

PRAYING IN THE BATHROOM AT THE
FIRST HOUR OF PRAYER

The first hour of prayer in the day is 6 a.m. in the morning. It is the beginning of the day watches also. It is the source of the watches of the day, even though the day dawns at 12 midnight. Prayer done at the first hour of 6 a.m. should focus on sanctifying the spirit, soul and body from every contamination of the night. Use the act of pouring water on your body to ask God to remove, by the water of His Word, every pollution in your system. This is time to believe God for the restoration of your glory. It is time to redeem everything the enemy may have stolen from you in the previous day. It is time to release the first arrows of war from the womb of the morning.

Make a proclamation from Psalm 19:1–6, *"The heavens declare the glory of God; the skies proclaim the work of his hands. Day after day they pour forth speech; night after night they reveal knowledge. They have no speech, they use no words; no sound is heard from them. Yet their voice goes out into all the earth, their words to the ends of the world. In the heavens God has pitched a tent for the sun. It is like a bridegroom coming out of his chamber, like a champion rejoicing to run his course. It rises at one end of the heavens and makes its circuit to the other; nothing is deprived of its warmth."*

Command the heavens to declare the glory of God over your life. Demand that they will speak of beauty and breakthroughs over your family and over your nation. Pray that all the blessings God has set for you that day in the tabernacles of the sun will be released. Declare that the day will usher you into the fulfilment of your destiny as the sun, like a bridegroom, comes out of his chamber and rejoices like a strongman to run its race. Pray that nothing that concerns you will be hidden from the sun as it undertakes its circuit for the day. Proclaim the words of Psalm 121:6-8, *"The sun shall not smite thee by day, nor the moon by night. The LORD shall preserve thee from all evil: he shall preserve thy soul. The LORD shall preserve thy going out and thy coming in from this time forth, and even for evermore."*

The first hour of prayer is a time to ask God to remove every stumbling block laid as a snare at the gates of the day. It is a time to sanctify the rest of the day at this altar of sanctification.

PRAYING IN THE BATHROOM AT THE THIRD HOUR OF PRAYER

The third hour of prayer is 9 a.m. in the morning. It was at this time that the Holy Spirit descended on the disciples at Pentecost. *"When the day of Pentecost came, they were all together in one place. Suddenly a sound like the blowing of a violent wind came from heaven and filled the whole house where they*

were sitting. They saw what seemed to be tongues of fire that separated and came to rest on each of them. All of them were filled with the Holy Spirit and began to speak in other tongues as the Spirit enabled them" (Acts 2:1-4).

When the people of Jerusalem thought that those who spoke in tongues at 9 a.m. were drunk, Peter responded to the criticism by saying: *"For these are not drunken, as ye suppose, seeing it is but the third hour of the day. But this is that which was spoken by the prophet Joel; And it shall come to pass in the last days, saith God, I will pour out of my Spirit upon all flesh: and your sons and your daughters shall prophesy, and your young men shall see visions, and your old men shall dream dreams: And on my servants and on my handmaidens I will pour out in those days of my Spirit; and they shall prophesy"* (Acts 2:15-18).

Praying in the bathroom at the third hour of prayer should lead to the invocation of the power of the Holy Spirit. Those who desire the baptism of the Holy Spirit with the initial evidence of speaking in tongues can actually be baptized in the bathroom. God will pour out his Spirit on all flesh at the altar of the bathroom. Our sons and daughters will activate the gift of prophecy in the bathroom. They will actually prophesy as the Lord envelops them with His glory at this altar of revival. The same is true for the young men and the old men who will see visions and dreams, respectively.

The third hour is a time to believe God for notable miracles. It was at this time that the notable miracle of the healing of the lame man at the Beautiful Gate was done. *"One day Peter and John were going up to the temple at the time of prayer at three in the afternoon. Now a man who was lame from birth was being carried to the temple gate called Beautiful, where he was put every day to beg from those going into the temple courts. When he saw Peter and John about to enter, he asked them for money. Peter looked straight at him, as did John. Then Peter said, "Look at us!" So the man gave them his attention, expecting to get something from them. Then Peter said, "Silver or gold I do not have, but what I do have I give you. In the name of Jesus Christ of Nazareth, walk." Taking him by the right hand, he helped him up, and instantly the man's feet and ankles became strong. He jumped to his feet and began to walk. Then he went with them into the temple courts, walking and jumping, and praising God"* (Acts 3: 1-8).

Many people testify to being healed in the bathroom. A woman whose husband had a terminal disease was brought home from the hospital when the doctors said there was nothing more they could do to preserve his life.

She entered the bathroom, stripped herself naked and cried to the Lord in her bathtub. She received an instant miracle as her husband recovered mysteriously.

The angels of the waters are still available to stir up the sanctified healing waters in your bathroom. Remember the man who had been paralysed for thirty-eight years at the pool of Bethesda. John 5: 2- 4 describes how people like him waited for an angel to stir the water to activate its healing virtues. *"Now there is in Jerusalem near the Sheep Gate a pool, which in Aramaic is called Bethesda and which is surrounded by five covered colonnades. Here a great number of disabled people used to lie the blind, the lame, the paralyzed. From time to time an angel of the Lord would come down and stir up the waters. The first one into the pool after each such disturbance would be cured of whatever disease they had."*

Although the paralytic man complained that he had no one to throw him into the pool when the water is stirred, Jesus still healed him while he was at the poolside. The lesson here is clear: the Lord Jesus, the Holy Spirit and the ministering angels are still waiting by the side of consecrated water bodies to activate the healing anointing. Your bathroom can be consecrated as an altar for the healing of infirmities, especially at the third hour of prayer, when the man at the Beautiful Gate was healed and when the people of God experienced the baptism of the Holy Spirit.

PRAYING IN THE BATHROOM AT THE SIXTH HOUR

The sixth hour of prayer is 12 noon. It is the very sensitive time of midday. There is a spirit of tiredness that envelops people at this time. The sun is usually hottest at the sixth hour. The atmosphere is so hot and humid that people are usually weary. Jesus met the woman of Samaria at the well during the sixth hour. *"Now he had to go through Samaria. So he came to a town in Samaria called Sychar, near the plot of ground Jacob had given to his son Joseph. Jacob's well was there, and Jesus, tired as he was from the journey, sat down by the well. It was about noon. When a Samaritan woman came to draw water, Jesus said to her, "Will you give me a drink?"* (John 4:4-7)

The fact that even Jesus was "wearied" at this time indicates why it will not be out of place to take a strategic bath at 12 noon for the purpose of dealing with the satanic forces that prowl at the sixth hour. Psalm 91: 5-6 talks about deliverance from the destruction that lays waste at noonday. *"You will not fear the terror of night, nor the arrow that flies by day, nor the pestilence that stalks in the darkness, nor the plague that destroys at midday".*

Apart from the fact that a bath at the sixth hour of weariness will refresh you, it will also afford you an opportunity to deal with the destruction that lays waste at noonday.

- **Pray that Persecutors of the Church will become Preachers of the Word.** It was at midday that Saul was arrested when he went to Damascus to arrest Christians. *"On one of these journeys I was going to Damascus with the authority and commission of the chief priests. About noon, King Agrippa, as I was on the road, I saw a light from heaven, brighter than the sun, blazing around me and my companions. We all fell to the ground, and I heard a voice saying to me in Aramaic 'Saul, Saul, why do you persecute me? It is hard for you to kick against the goads"* (Acts 26:12-14).

- **Pray that those in Trouble will Receive Help in the Heat.** It was at midday that the people of Jabesh Gilead received help from Saul when Nahash the serpent threatened to pluck out their right eyes if they did not enter into a covenant with him. *"They told the messengers who had come, 'Say to the men of Jabesh Gilead, By the time the sun is hot tomorrow, you will be rescued.' When the messengers went and reported this to the men of Jabesh, they were elated"* (1Samuel 11:9)

- **Pray for Angelic Visitations and Covenant Blessings.** It was at the sixth hour of midday that angels visited and released the covenant blessing of children to Abraham and Sarah. *"And the LORD appeared unto him in the plains of Mamre: and he sat in the tent door in the heat of the* *day; And he lift up his eyes and looked, and, lo, three men stood by him: and when he saw them, he ran to meet them from the tent door, and bowed himself toward the ground... And they said unto him, Where is Sarah thy wife? And he said, Behold, in the tent. And he said, I will certainly return unto thee according to the time of life; and, lo, Sarah thy wife shall have a son. And Sarah heard it in the tent door, which was behind him"* (Genesis 18:1-2, 9-10).

- **Pray for the Transformation of your Mindset.** It was at the seaside town of Joppa that Peter had a vision of someone calling him to kill and eat animals that Jews would usually consider unclean. This vision compelled Peter to minister to Gentiles who received the Lord, were baptized in the Holy Ghost and with water. *"About noon the following day as they were on their journey and approaching the city, Peter went up on the roof to pray. He became hungry and wanted something to eat, and while the meal was being prepared, he fell into a trance. He saw heaven opened and something like a large sheet being let down to earth by its four corners. It contained all kinds of four-footed animals, as well as reptiles and birds. Then a voice told him, 'Get up, Peter. Kill and eat.' 'Surely not, Lord!' Peter replied. 'I have never eaten anything impure or unclean.' The voice spoke to him a second time, 'Do not call anything impure that God has made clean.' This happened three times, and immediately the sheet was taken back to heaven. While Peter was wondering about the meaning of the vision, the men sent by Cornelius found out where Simon's house was and stopped at the gate. They called out, asking if Simon who was known as Peter was staying there. While Peter was still thinking about the vision, the Spirit said to him, 'Simon, three men are looking for you. So get up and go downstairs. Do not hesitate to go with them, for I have sent them'"* (Acts 10:9-20).

The sixth hour is break time in most nations. This means that even those at work can take out time to take a strategic bath and pray in the bathroom if their offices have facilities for this purpose.

PRAYING IN THE BATHROOM AT THE NINTH HOUR

The ninth hour is the time of 3 p.m. It was at this time that Jesus gave up the Ghost on the Cross. There was total darkness between the sixth and the ninth hours. Just at the point Jesus gave up the Ghost; the veil of the temple was torn from top to bottom. *"It was now about noon, and darkness came over the whole land until three in the afternoon, for the sun stopped shining. And the curtain of the temple was torn in two. Jesus called out with a loud voice, 'Father, into your hands I commit my spirit.' When he had said this, he breathed his last. The centurion, seeing what had happened, praised God and said, 'Surely this was a righteous man'"* (Luke 23:44- 47).

The ninth hour is a time to release strategic darkness in the kingdom of darkness. The essence is to ensure that they are confused about Gods original plans and purposes. It is a good time to ask God to tear the veils that hinder access to God and his prophetic agenda. Make a proclamation from Isaiah 25:7-8, *"On this mountain he will destroy the shroud that enfolds all peoples, the sheet that covers all nations; he will swallow up death forever. The Sovereign LORD will wipe away the tears from all faces; he will remove his people's disgrace from all the earth. The LORD has spoken."*

Pray that God will destroy the covering cast over all people. Ask Him to tear the veil that is spread over nations. Declare that God will swallow up death forever, that He will wipe away tears from all faces and take away all insults and mockery. All these will culminate into manifestation of God's glory as indicated in Isaiah 25:6, *"On this mountain the LORD Almighty will prepare a feast of rich food for all peoples, a banquet of aged wine the best of meats and the finest of wines."*

Remember that Cornelius, a centurion of the Italian Regiment, a generous and devout man who feared God, received a vision to send for Peter where he lodged at the sea-side town of Joppa at the ninth hour. *"At Caesarea there was a man named Cornelius, a centurion in what was known as the Italian*

Regiment. He and all his family were devout and God-fearing; he gave generously to those in need and prayed to God regularly. One day at about three in the afternoon he had a vision. He distinctly saw an angel of God, who came to him and said, 'Cornelius!' Cornelius stared at him in fear. 'What is it, Lord?' he asked. The angel answered, 'Your prayers and gifts to the poor have come up as a memorial offering before God. Now send men to Joppa to bring back a man named Simon who is called Peter. He is staying with Simon the tanner, whose house is by the sea.' When the angel who spoke to him had gone, Cornelius called two of his servants and a devout soldier who was one of his attendants. He told them everything that had happened and sent them to Joppa" (Acts 10:1-8).

Pray that the Cornelius around you will also have angelic visitations and directions. There are many such men who are generous, devout and prayerful, who do not yet know the Lord Jesus. Ask God to send knowledgeable apostles to tell them what to do to truly belong to God's Kingdom.

It is amazing that God asked Cornelius to send for Peter who was *"lodging with Simon, a tanner whose house is by the sea"* at the ninth hour. It is even more amazing that *"Peter went up to the housetop"* overlooking the sea *"to pray about the sixth hour"* and received the vision and instruction that compelled him to go and minister to Cornelius, a Gentile, in whose house he would never have entered to speak the Word of God.

PRAYING IN THE BATHROOM AT OTHERS TIMES OF PRAYER

There are other times of prayer which we cannot deal with in detail here. The twelfth hour is the time of 6 p.m. It is the source of the watches of the night. There is also 12 midnight which is equally strategic as we indicated in our book *The Power of Praying at Midnight*. It is a time when death can be exchanged for life. It is a time of praise and worship which has the capacity to release spiritual earthquakes that will set captives free. *"When he received these orders, he put them in the inner cell and fastened their feet in the stocks.*

About midnight Paul and Silas were praying and singing hymns to God, and the other prisoners were listening to them. Suddenly there was such a violent earthquake that the foundations of the prison were shaken. At once all the prison doors flew open, and everyone's chains came loose. The jailer woke up, and when he saw the prison doors open, he drew his sword and was about to kill himself because he thought the prisoners had escaped. But Paul shouted, 'Don't harm yourself! We are all here!' The jailer called for lights, rushed in and fell trembling before Paul

and Silas. He then brought them out and asked, 'Sirs, what must I do to be saved?' They replied, 'Believe in the Lord Jesus, and you will be saved you and your household.' Then they spoke the word of the Lord to him and to all the others in his house. At that hour of the night the jailer took them and washed their wounds; then immediately he and all his household were baptized. The jailer brought them into his house and set a meal before them; he was filled with joy because he had come to believe in God he and his whole household" (Acts 16:25-34).

You may not be able to take a bath and pray at all the times of prayer listed above. It is important, however, to note that bath time can be structured to synchronise with the Biblical hours of prayer. Furthermore, the type of prayer rendered at specific times in the bathroom can be based on the revelation of the Biblical events that happened at the particular hours of prayer. Bath time can become a powerful time of prayer and supplication. It can become a purposeful time of intercession for your family, the church and the nations.

17
SPIRITUAL BREAKTHROUGHS
IN THE BATHROOM

17

Spiritual Breakthroughs in the Bathroom

"Running water does not need a hole" – **Ghanaian Proverb.**

The presence of the Holy Spirit and angels around water bodies automatically indicates that the bathroom will always be a place of beauty and breakthroughs. The potentials for spiritual encounters are so great around consecrated water that one should not be surprised about miraculous experiences in the bathroom. Testimonies abound on the glorious things God has done for those that trust in Him as they took their baths. Let us examine some of them as we continue to explore the amazing revelation of the prophetic significance of the bathroom.

BREAKTHROUGH OF RESOURCES AND INTERNATIONAL OPEN DOORS IN THE BATHROOM

A friend on Facebook, Ethel Abe, testifies of the wonderful encounters she and her husband experienced in the bathroom. According to Ethel, God gave them a mandate to organise a National Day of Thanksgiving in 2006. Unfortunately, they had no financial resources to execute this divine assignment. It was a dilemma to have a divine mandate without the resources to fulfil it. Ethel says that *"one morning, I went to the bathroom and suddenly I said out of my mouth, 'My resources are with you.'"* This was the visionary prophesying to herself by the Word of the Lord. Ethel quickly rushed out of the bathroom and repeated the same words to her husband. God honoured His Word as He provided over twelve million Naira for the execution of the National Day of Thanksgiving. Ethel and her husband discovered an amazing depth of God's resources for doing His bidding daily.

Secondly, Ethel's husband also had his own personal encounter in the bathroom in 2007. It was while at this altar of revelation that he heard God say: *"I called you Isaac and not Idowu that they call you."* Mr. Abe promptly changed his name to Isaac and immediately noticed a radical transformation in his ministry.

Ethel notes that before her husband's change of name, *"He knew of his international ministry, but all attempts to actualise it failed even after travelling to some countries."* But immediately he obeyed the Lord and changed his name from Idowu to Isaac, the doors of ministry outside Nigeria opened in an amazing and consistent way. Isaiah 62:2-5 says, *"The nations will see your vindication, and all kings your glory; you will be called by a new name that the mouth of the LORD will bestow. You will be a crown of splendour in the LORD's hand, a royal diadem in the hand of your God. No longer will they call you Deserted, or name your land Desolate. But you will be called Hephzibah and your land Beulah; for the LORD will take delight in you, and your land will be married. As a young man marries a young woman, so will your Builder marry you; as a bridegroom rejoices over his bride, so will your God rejoice over you."*

DIVINE DELIVERANCE IN THE BATHROOM

Ukpai Uwaka Kalu was delivered from death in the bathroom. The most touching moments of his life often happened in the bathroom. Ukpai always had a new song spring out from his lips in the bathroom. Whenever this happened, he felt the strong hand of the Lord upon him with the consequence of spiritual upliftment.

In March 1999, Upkai slipped off the bathtub and hit his leg against a sharp object on the tile. This accident resulted in a sharp and deep cut which began to bleed profusely. The cut was so deep that the bone on his leg was clearly exposed. Ukpai lay down on the ground unable to stand, with blood flowing profusely. In this critical situation, with no one to help him, a new song began to proceed from his mouth. He struggled to sing in this state of adversity. The more Ukpai sang, the more he was energised and strengthened. He was eventually able to get up on his own from the floor, thankful that the Holy Spirit enabled him to overcome this life-threatening challenge.

CHARACTER TRANSFORMATION IN THE BATHROOM

The greatest spiritual breakthrough everyone should desire to have in the bathroom is character transformation. Carnal minds can be transformed by the mind of Christ as you minister to the Lord and to yourself at the altar of sanctification.

Dr. Ben Carson, who had a problem with anger in his youth, also had a mighty encounter with the Lord in the bathroom that helped him to radically modify his behaviour. One day, while in ninth grade, Carson had a small argument with Bob his friend. It was over what constituted good music on the transistor radio. The argument seemed like a minor and harmless disagreement between friends. But it exposed the terrible rage in Carson. As he himself testified, *"Grabbing the camping knife I carried in my back pocket, I snapped it open and lunged for the boy who had been my friend. With all the power of my young muscles, I thrust the knife toward his belly. The knife hit his big, heavy belt buckle with such force that the blade snapped and dropped to the ground. I stared at the broken blade and went weak. I had almost killed my friend."*

Realising what had happened, Carson muttered a weak "I'm sorry". dropped the handle of the broken knife and ran home. The house was empty when he got home. Instinctively, Carson "raced to the bathroom", locked the door and was alone. He hung on the edge of the bathtub, his *"long legs stretching across the linoleum, bumping against the sink."* His mind was racing back and forth. He realised that he could have actually killed his friend.

"This is crazy," he mumbled to himself in the quiet atmosphere of the bathroom. *"I must be crazy. Sane people don't try to kill their friends."* Suddenly, Carson realised that even though he was doing well at school, anger could scuttle his desire to be a doctor – a passion that had been with him since he was eight years old.

It was in the bathroom that Carson realised that he could not handle his anger problem alone, that he needed someone greater than him to deal with the rage within. This realisation led him to pray the way his mother had taught him. *"Lord",* he whispered, *"you have to take this temper from me. If you don't, I'll never be free from it. I'll end up doing things a lot worse than trying to stab one of my best friends."*

Ben Carson was in the bathroom, an altar of sanctification. The Holy Spirit was there and the angels were probably there also. He cried for God to change him. *"You can change me,"* he said. *"You can free me forever from this destructive personality trait."* In tears, with his nose running, Carson continued to plead with God in the bathroom. *"You've promised that if we come to you and ask something in faith, that you'll do it... If you don't do this for me, God, I've got no place else to go."*

At some point, Carson left the bathroom "long enough to grab a Bible". He opened it instinctively when he returned to Proverbs 16:32 which says, *"He who is slow to anger is better than the mighty, and he who rules his spirit than he who takes a city."* According to Carson, *"My lips moved wordlessly as I continued to read. I felt as though the verses had been written just for me. The words of Proverbs condemned me, but they also gave me hope. After a while peace began to fill my mind. My hands stopped shaking. The tears stopped. During those hours alone in the bathroom, something happened to me. God heard my deep cries of anguish. A feeling of lightness flowed over me, and I knew a change of heart had taken place. I felt different. I was different. At last I stood up, placed the Bible on the edge of the tub and went to the sink. I washed my face and hands and straightened my clothes. Then, I walked out of the bathroom a changed young man. 'My temper will never control me again, I told myself. Never again, I am free.'* To conclude his testimony of amazing salvation and freedom from anger, Carson notes that *'During those hours in the bathroom I also came to realise that if people could make me angry they could control me. Why should I give someone else such power over my life?'"*

You too can be set free. You can experience freedom from any bondage, be it a sexual, drug or character bondage. Run to the altar in your bathroom. Take the water of God's Word with you. Carson was able to overcome with the water of God's Word in the Bible. He read the Scripture relevant to dealing with his temper tantrum. He received a miracle of character transformation in the bathroom and went on to become the doctor he always wanted to be. You can overcome any bondage to become all that God wants you to be. *"The LORD is compassionate and gracious; slow to anger, abounding in love. He will not always accuse, nor will he harbour his anger forever; he does not treat us as our sins deserve or repay us according to our iniquities. For as high as the heavens are above the earth, so great is his love for those who fear him; as far as the east is from the west, so far has he removed our transgressions from us. As a father has compassion on his children, so the LORD has compassion on those who fear him; for he knows how we are formed, he remembers that we are dust"* (Psalm 103:8-14).

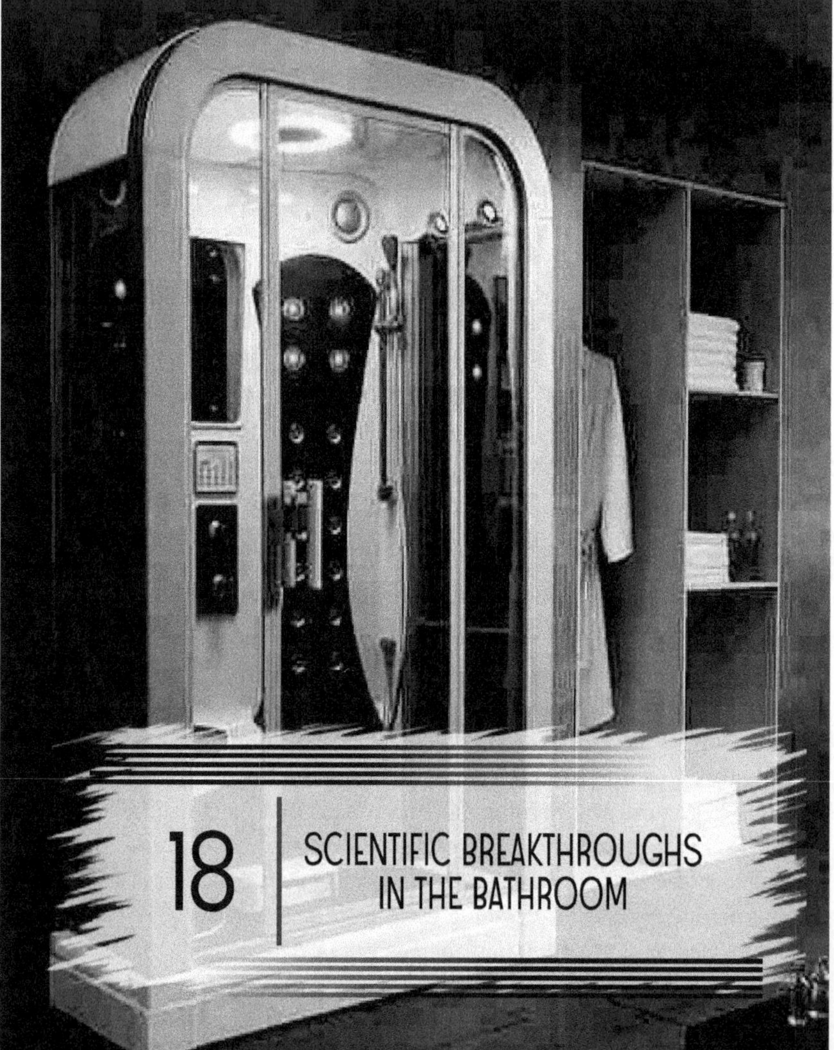

18 | SCIENTIFIC BREAKTHROUGHS IN THE BATHROOM

18
Scientific Breakthroughs in the Bathroom

"He who wishes to pick stones from the bottom of a river must be prepared to get wet" – **Nigerian Proverb.**

There is a glory to be unleashed in the bathroom which will affect every aspect of life. As we noted earlier, the consecrated bathroom will become a spiritual and intellectual magnet for all who desire deeper dimensions of fellowship with God and with their intellect.

Taking a bath will go beyond the desire to physically clean your body. It would include the necessity to seek for solutions to scientific problems. The bathroom will become a vital place for receiving inspiration for decoding hard sentences. This may sound preposterous to those who are still ignorant of the fact that God works in mysterious ways His wonders to perform. It will sound like madness to the humanists and atheists who deny the existence of God. The reality, however, is that the bathroom has always been an altar of revelation for people with fertile imaginations.

ACTIVATING THE SCIENCE OF DESIGNS IN THE BATHROOM

In this era of "boundless ingenuity", there can be no better theatre for receiving models than in the bathroom. Those whose names are written in the Lamb's Book of Life in Heaven will be connected to heavenly patterns as they activate their creative faculties in the bathroom. They will receive engineering models, architectural designs and incredible revelations that can be replicated on earth to solve chronic problems.

This is already happening, but the intensity and volume will increase in the days to come. Engineer Irisominabo testified that most of his engineering designs are received and perfected in the bathroom. He is engaged in major construction projects for the government and for private organisations. For this busy engineer, going to the bathroom is not just a matter of cleaning his body or removing waste matter. Those who see him walk into the bathroom may be deceived to think that he is going in there to do what they go to the toilet to do. But they are wrong. Engineer Irisominabo goes to the bathroom to receive divine inspiration to create designs.

Are you an architect or an engineer? Are you a graphic artist? Then begin to see your job in a new context. Your task can be easier if you depend on the divine presence in your bathroom. Modern-day architects must begin to conceive the type of bathrooms that can accommodate strategic desktop computers and drawing boards. Already, aqua-notes have been invented to facilitate the quick documentation of divine ideas received in the bathroom. As we noted earlier, the aqua-notes are waterproof in nature. People with creative imaginations no longer need to worry about the loss of their fresh ideas to wet pads and forgetful memories.

ARCHIMEDES' DISCOVERY OF THE LAW OF BUOYANCY IN THE BATHROOM

The law of buoyancy, which is fundamental to the design of ocean liners and other boats, was discovered in the bathroom by Archimedes, a second-century mathematician from Syracuse, Sicily. Archimedes was a man of "boundless ingenuity". He laid down the basic principles of hydrostatics in his book *On Floating Bodies*. The process by which he discovered the science of hydrostatics and particularly the law of buoyancy had something to do with taking a bath.

King Hiero of Sicily commissioned a goldsmith to design and construct a new golden royal crown. After the crown was designed and delivered, Hiero suspected that the goldsmith must have cheated him by mixing silver and gold to achieve the required weight of the crown. Hiero needed someone to determine the "purity of the crown" without tearing it apart, and he turned to Archimedes for help.

The challenge before Archimedes was how to determine whether the goldsmith used pure gold to construct the crown or mixed it with silver. This difficult challenge was, however, resolved by a divine inspiration Archimedes received while taking a bath.

Archimedes discovered that as he lowered himself into the bath, water overflowed from the bathtub. This instantly made him realise that he could determine the weight or density of the crown by simply measuring the volume or amount of water it displaces when lowered in water.

Ecstatic and exhilarated, Archimedes ran out naked from the bathroom shouting, "Eureka! Eureka!" This means, "I have found it! I have found it!"

Archimedes helped king Hiero to prove that he had indeed been cheated by the goldsmith. The so called golden crown was not all golden after all. The designer had mixed silver and gold, hoping that his despicable act will not be discovered by the king or anyone else.

THE ARCHIMEDES' PRINCIPLE

The law of buoyancy discovered in the bathroom is also called Archimedes' principle, after the name of its author. It is the subject of Proposition 5 in Archimedes' treatise *On Floating Bodies*. It states that *"any floating object displaced its own weight of fluid."* When applied to liquids and gases, the Archimedes' principle stated in terms of forces indicates that *"any object, wholly or partially immersed in fluid, is buoyed up by a force equal to the weight of the fluid displaced by the object."* In other words, *"for a soaked object, the volume of the displaced fluid is the volume of the object and for a floating object on a liquid, the weight of the displaced liquid is the weight of the object."*

If the basic principle of hydrostatics were discovered by chance in the bathroom, you can imagine how many more discoveries scientists can make at this altar of revelation if they fully appreciate the prophetic significance of the bathroom and the glory of divine presence there.

WHY THE BATHROOM WILL CONTINUE TO BE A PLACE OF INSPIRATION FOR SCIENTIFIC BREAKTHROUGHS

The relationship between taking a bath and activating intellectual and spiritual breakthroughs in the bathroom is not difficult to understand. The brain is the most important part of the body for intellectual activities. It contains more water than many parts of the human body.

WATER CONTENT OF SOME BODY PARTS

S/N	Body Part	Water Content
1.	Brain	90%
2.	Blood	83%
3.	Muscles	75%
4.	Bones	22%

Notice that 90% of the brain is made up of water. It is possible that when consecrated water with divine presence falls on the body, it activates the brain in such a way that spiritual and scientific breakthroughs become possible. Deep will always call for deep. How else can we explain the fact that most people get inspired in the bathroom in the way they are not outside? The water in the brain may be responding to the water of God's Word for the purpose of creativity.

There is no doubt that the presence of the Holy Spirit in the bathroom activates deeper dimensions of inspiration. Whenever the Holy Spirit hovers over water, creativity and innovation becomes inevitable, just as it was at the beginning of the creative process of Genesis 1:1-3. *"In the beginning God created the heaven and the earth. And the earth was without form and void. And darkness was upon the face of the deep. And the Spirit of God moved upon the face of the waters. And God said, let there be light: and there was light."*

19 | HEALING AND DELIVERANCE BREAKTHROUGH IN THE BATHROOM

19

Healing and Deliverance Breakthrough in the Bathroom

The relationship between consecrated water and healing is amply demonstrated in Scripture. Naaman the leper was healed when he dipped himself seven times in the River Jordan as he was instructed by Elisha the prophet. The pool of Bethesda was consecrated for the healing of infirmities. *"Now there is at Jerusalem by the sheep market a pool, which is called in the Hebrew tongue Bethesda, having five porches. In these lay a great multitude of impotent folk, of blind, halt, withered, waiting for the moving of the water. For an angel went down at a certain season into the pool, and troubled the water: whosoever then first after the troubling of the water stepped in was made whole of whatsoever disease he had"* (John 5:2-4).

Several occult churches have perverted the use of water as a token of healing. Some sell what they call "holy water", while others divert people's attention from putting their faith in God and the water of His Word. The drive to merchandise God's gift compel them to manipulate people to put their faith in tokens rather than in God.

Nevertheless, we must avoid the tendency to reject a revelation because it has been perverted. The presence of a counterfeit strongly suggests that there is an original. We must not throw the baby and the bathing water merely because a particular revelation of God's manifestation on earth has been bastardised. The bathroom is indeed a place of healing and deliverance. Several people have testified of being healed and delivered as they were taking their bath. In chapter one of this book, we recounted Theresa's testimony. The Lord did a surgical operation on her that led to the removal of a massive fibroid from her womb.

BREAKTHROUGH OF PREGNANCY AND DELIVERY OF TWINS

Evangelist Nkechi Igbanibo of Battle Axe Ministries in Port Harcourt, Nigeria tells the wonderful encounter of a supposedly barren husband and wife in the bathroom that led to the birth of twins.

A woman who could not have a baby for eight years after marriage came to Evangelist Igbanibo for help. She and her husband had earlier visited many pastors and prophets in search of children to no avail. It seemed as if God no longer answered prayers. Reflecting on what the Lord would have them do, Igbanibo received a seemingly strange word from the Lord for them. *"My daughter, tell her to be sensitive to the Holy Spirit anytime she enters her bathroom, because that is where God will visit her."*

Seven days after receiving the word of the Lord, the lady was taking a bath with her husband when the Lord instructed her to tell her husband to read 2Kings 2:19-22, *"And the men of the city said unto Elisha, Behold, I pray thee, the situation of this city is pleasant, as my lord seeth: but the water is naught, and the ground barren. And he said, Bring me a new cruse, and put salt therein. And they brought it to him. And he went forth unto the spring of the waters, and cast the salt in there, and said, Thus saith the LORD, I have healed these waters; there shall not be from thence any more death or barren land. So the waters were healed unto this day, according to the saying of Elisha which he spake"* (2 Kings 2:19-22).

God further instructed this lady to tell her husband to do a prophetic action similar to the one Elisha the prophet did to bring healing to the land

and the waters of Jericho. He was commanded to put salt in a water-filled bowl and sprinkle it on their bed. He was also commanded to pray for the yoke of barrenness to be broken in his family. Miraculously, his wife became pregnant two months after he obeyed these seemingly strange instructions. Nine months later, she delivered a set of twins, a boy and a girl.

Obedience to divine instructions is vital for receiving miraculous breakthroughs. Many people have missed because of doubt and disobedience. They failed to understand that often times the prophetic does not conform to traditions. God is still calling us to come and reason with him. *"Come now, and let us reason together, saith the LORD: though your sins be as scarlet, they shall be as white as snow; though they be red like crimson, they shall be as wool. If ye be willing and obedient, ye shall eat the good of the land: But if ye refuse and rebel, ye shall be devoured with the sword: for the mouth of the LORD hath spoken it"* (Isaiah 1:18-20).

THE FLOOD LIGHT THAT BROUGHT DELIVERANCE

Evangelist Nkechi Igbanibo's elder brother who lives in Abuja was terribly sick. He was admitted in a hospital in Abuja for two weeks, but every effort to cure him failed. His mother requested that he should be brought back home to Asaba. She and her prayer partners organized a seven-day night vigil on his behalf.

On the fourth day of their prayer-vigil, the sick man requested to be taken to the bathroom to answer the call of nature. Assisted by his wife, they got to the bathroom to witness a strange encounter. As he made very great effort to ease himself, a powerful flood light penetrated the bathroom from outside. It was as though someone was shining a mighty flood light on them. Instinctively, husband and wife shouted "who are you? Put off the light".

On hearing their shout, other members of the family rushed into the bathroom to see what was happening. To their amazement, the light the sick man and his wife wanted to put off was actually a divine light sent to heal and deliver them. Evangelist Nkechi Igbanibo's brother was healed instantly. The man who needed the help of his wife to enter the bathroom, walked out unaided. God's searchlight had instantly healed him in the bathroom. His sickness disappeared and the night vigils organised on his behalf also ended.

What a mighty God we serve! His promises of healing and deliverance are still available for those who trust in Him. *"And now my soul is poured out upon me; the days of affliction have taken hold upon me. My bones are pierced in me in the night season: and my sinews take no rest"* (Job 30:16-17).

Remember the prophetic word on end time bathrooms, The Word of the Lord will come to you in the bathroom as never before. You will hear the Lord saying, "This is the way to go." There will be great angelic visitations in the bathroom. There will be miraculous encounters as the shower runs its healing virtues on your spirit, soul and body. The depressed will be delivered, the sick will be healed, and the oppressed will be set free in the bathroom. A mighty miraculous wave will be seen in this hitherto ordinary place with a new extraordinary significance. The consecrated bathroom will become a spiritual magnet for all who desire a deeper dimension of fellowship with God. Going to the bathroom will no longer be a routine act. It will become a special spiritual phenomenon. Taking a bath will go beyond the desire of people to physically clean their bodies. It will include a passion to see old mind sets changed into transformed outlooks. The physical washing with water will become the prophetic action that will instigate the washing of the mind by the water of the Word. Don't be surprised if the Holy Spirit propels you to take a bath even when you have no need for physical cleansing. Do not resist the prompting to fellowship with the Lord at the altar of your bathroom.

STEVE OGAN

KISS ME IN THE KITCHEN

MINISTERING AS A PRIEST
AT THE ALTAR OF THE KITCHEN

STEVE OGAN
PROPHETIC
MARRIAGE
Marriage and
Other Covenants
in God's Plan
for the Nations

STEVE OGAN

QUIPS & QUOTES ABOUT KISSES & KITCHENS

FOR LOVERS WHO COOK AND THOSE WHO EAT WHAT THEY COOK

How to
BEAT
YOUR
Husband
Towards A
SUCCESSFUL
CHRISTIAN
Family
STEVE OGAN

HOW TO
BEAT
YOUR
Wife
Towards A
SUCCESSFUL
CHRISTIAN
Family
STEVE OGAN

How To
BEAT
your WIFE II
STEVE OGAN
AWARD WINNING AUTHOR OF 'HOW TO BEAT YOUR HUSBAND'
& 'HOW TO BEAT YOUR WIFE'

How to
BEAT your
HUSBAND II
STEVE OGAN
AWARD WINNING AUTHOR OF 'HOW TO BEAT YOUR WIFE'
& 'HOW TO BEAT YOUR HUSBAND'

HORRORS & HASSLES of HELL
STEVE OGAN

HOLINESS and HIGH CALLINGS of HEAVEN
STEVE OGAN

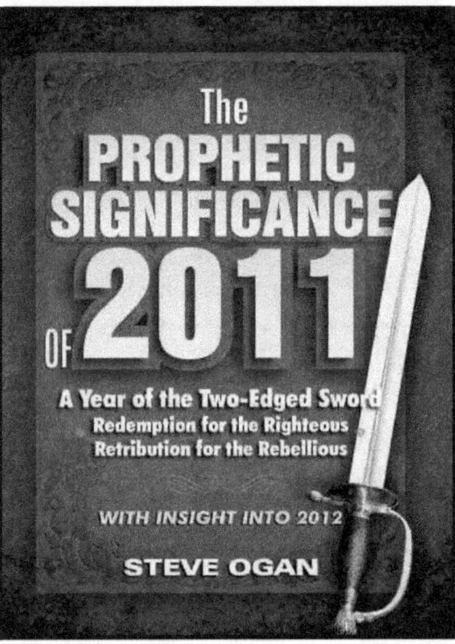
The
PROPHETIC SIGNIFICANCE
OF 2011
A Year of the Two-Edged Sword
Redemption for the Righteous
Retribution for the Rebellious
WITH INSIGHT INTO 2012
STEVE OGAN

CONTENDING WITH
INTELLECTUAL
IDOLATRY
AND
MORAL DECAY
Understanding and Overcoming
the Anti-Christian Worldview
STEVE OGAN

OTHER MARRIAGE RELATED BOOKS BY AUTHOR

1. How to Beat Your In-laws
2. How to Beat Your Children
3. Holy Rod: Parents and the Discipline of Children
4. Raising Rainbow-Type Family Altars
5. Your Honeymoon Can Last Forever
6. Dealing with Incompatibility in Your Marriage
7. Battle For Marriage and Family Life
8. Starting Rainbow Kitchen Initiatives.
9. Making Miracles in Your Marriage
10. Humanism and Attacks on the Family
11. Wow, This Is It! Knowing God's Will in Choosing a Life Partner
12. Waging War with Widows
13. Clean Courtship for Intending Couples.
14. You Can Fly Like the Eagle
15. You're Single Not Stupid I
16. You're Single Not Stupid II
17. You're Single Not Stupid III
18. Ethics and Pitfalls of Marriage Counselling
19. Theories and Therapies of Marriage Counselling
20. Training for Pastors and Marriage Counsellors (TPMC Basic Manual)
21. Training for Pastors and Marriage Counsellors (TPMC Intermediate Manual)
22. Professional Training for Marriage Counsellors (PTMC Advanced Manual)
23. The First Fundamental Principles of Marriage
24. Promise to Marry and Breach of Promise: The Legal Implication of not Fulfilling a Promise to Marry
25. Marah: Breaking the Bondage of Bitterness and Barrenness
26. The Requirement of Statutory Law Marriage in Nigeria
27. The Requirement of Customary Law Marriage in Nigeria